# Designs on
# the Public

KRISTINE F. MILLER

# Designs on the Public

## The Private Lives of New York's Public Spaces

University of Minnesota Press
Minneapolis
London

Photographs not otherwise credited were taken by
the author.

Published by the University of Minnesota Press
111 Third Avenue South, Suite 290
Minneapolis, MN 55401-2520
http://www.upress.umn.edu


Library of Congress Cataloging-in-Publication Data

Miller, Kristine F.
    Designs on the public : the private lives of
New York's public spaces / Kristine F. Miller.
        p. cm.
    Includes bibliographical references and index.
    ISBN: 978-0-8166-4909-9 (hc : alk. paper)
    ISBN-10: 0-8166-4909-X (hc : alk. paper)
    ISBN: 978-0-8166-4910-5 (pb : alk. paper)
    ISBN-10: 0-8166-4910-3 (pb : alk. paper)
    1. Public spaces—New York (State)—New York.
2. Architecture and society—New York (State)—New York.
3. Land use, Urban—New York (State)—New York. I. Title.
    NA9053.S6M55  2007
    711′.55097471—dc22

                                        2007023709


Printed in the United States of America on acid-free paper

The University of Minnesota is an equal-opportunity
educator and employer.


15  14  13  12  11  10  09  08  07
10  9  8  7  6  5  4  3  2  1

# Contents

# Acknowledgments

Many people helped with the research, writing, and rewriting of this book. The staff, students, and faculty of the Department of Landscape Architecture at the University of Minnesota were unfailingly supportive throughout the entire process. Early ideas about politics and public spaces took shape with the help of Vincent deBritto and Susan Buck-Morss. Katherine Solomonson and Doug Armato encouraged me to develop a group of essays, images, and questions into a set of connected cases.

Each chapter benefited from the insights of many readers. I am indebted to Juliette Cherbuliez, Anne Carter, Diane Brown, Michael Levine, Bill Taylor, Lance Neckar, and Marc Treib, who reviewed multiple versions of multiple chapters. Don Mitchell offered advice on the entire manuscript. Marcella Eaton, Kate Hopper, Lynn Staeheli, Lynda Schneekloth, Mark Battley, Heather Hewson, Samer Alatout, Denis Calis, Kathleen Christian, Elizabeth Lebas, Michel Conan, Anne Gardner, Lisa Disch, and Tom Fisher offered ideas at key points along the way.

Setha Low, Jane Jacobs, Jerold Kayden, Neil Selkirk, Chris Dunn, Mark Luehrs, Thomas Martin, Ted Zimmerman, Carrie Jacobs, Alex Marshall, and Pamela MacKinnon generously shared their expertise around particular cases and issues. Sallie Steele created the index. Generous funding from the University of Minnesota Grant-in-Aid of Research, Artistry, and Scholarship Program and the Dumbarton Oaks Garden and Landscape Studies Program supported the research for this book.

I am sincerely grateful for the encouragement of Donald and Gloria Miller, David Miller, Donald Miller, Diane McDonald, Mary Criddle, and Maureen Anderson.

ACKNOWLEDGMENTS

# Introduction
## What Is Public Space?

**We tend to think of public space** as having certain essential and obvious characteristics. We believe it is publicly owned, the opposite of private space. We believe it is open and accessible to everyone, where no one can be turned away. We imagine it as the setting for important civic events, where large groups of people come to celebrate, protest, and mourn. We see it as somehow part of democratic life—a place for speaking out and being heard.

We also think we know New York City. It seems uniquely familiar to us, even to those of us who don't live there or who have never visited and even before the intense television coverage of 9/11. New York's public spaces and public life have been portrayed in countless films, novels, television shows, photographs, and songs. We can all conjure up an image of New Year's Eve in Times Square, political speeches at City Hall, the handmade memorials near the World Trade Center site, crowds with their faces pressed up against television studio windows, the marathon, the Macy's Parade, and sidewalks packed with commuters and holiday shoppers. We imagine that public life in New York is somehow spontaneous and unregulated—perhaps even dangerous, or at least unpredictable.

But for all we think we know about a seemingly straightforward term such as *public space* and an iconic city like New York, their realities are much more complicated. In many instances they are not as we imagine them at all. The following chapters chronicle particular moments in the histories of six of New York's most famous public spaces. The stories show that public space is not a concrete reality but rather a tenuous condition. What we believe are its essential and enduring qualities—openness and accessibility, public ownership, and ties to democratic life—are at best temporary conditions, and more often are completely absent. Similarly, New York's public life is not spontaneous. It is bound by regulation and codes of conduct. These codes and regulations not only control what can happen on the streets and sidewalks, plazas and parks, but also who can be present there—in other words, who constitutes New York's public.

Physical barriers and controls on places, such as the fences and security checks at City Hall, seem the clearest form of restricting access to public spaces. Measures put in place purportedly to increase safety are the most obvious evidence that public spaces, as many currently exist, are not open and accessible. But what about a place such as Times Square, which is nothing more than streets and sidewalks? Couldn't anyone walk though Times Square today? While the streets and sidewalks of Times Square are full of people doing exactly that—walking —not to mention tourists taking in the cacophony of lights and sounds, the history of the transformation of Times Square tells a different story. Times Square may appear open, but controlling access to a public space can be accomplished by restricting who is there in the first place. These constraints can happen over long stretches of time and are therefore much more difficult to identify than police barricades. In Times Square the transformation of the public happened over nearly thirty years and involved condemnation and demolition, massive imaging campaigns, evictions, and a nearly complete recasting of who the real public of Times Square should be.

If public space as it exists today is not open and accessible to all, neither is it necessarily publicly owned. This book's second half describes three of New York's 503 Privately Owned Public Spaces (POPS), a growing category of public spaces across the United States and Canada.[1] In New York, POPS arose out of the 1961 New York City Zoning Resolution, which allowed developers to construct additional building floors if a public space was provided inside or in front of the building. The program was seen as a way that New York could get new, high-quality public spaces without spending city

INTRODUCTION

money. Sony Plaza, the former IBM Atrium, and the Atrium at Trump Tower are considered the jewels in the crown of the POPS program. Analysis of these three cases calls into question the degree to which these spaces are indeed open and accessible as well as challenges the purported benefits of such legal and financial trade-offs.

Also, public spaces are not inextricably tied to the practice of democracy—not even those spaces that are literally tied to important public buildings such as New York's City Hall. The front steps of City Hall, arguably the most important locale in the civic life of New York, represent an ideal design for a public space as a setting for democratic action. We may think that our right to speak freely in public space is guaranteed, but it is actually highly regulated and therefore contingent, as the history of the steps of City Hall during the Giuliani administration illustrates. Legal battles between Giuliani and a nonprofit group critical of his policies showed that even public spaces that would appear to be ideal platforms for political expression can be shut down through regulation.

Why is our commonsense definition of public space so far from reality? Part of the problem is our preoccupation with the enduring physical qualities of public spaces: we tend to spend more time thinking about the places themselves. This preoccupation is particularly prevalent in design history and criticism. By focusing on the physical and the concrete, we often ignore nonphysical qualities—legal, economic, political, aesthetic—all of which affect a public space. Public spaces do not exist as static physical entities but are constellations of ideas, actions, and environments.

If public space is not as we imagine it, what should it be? Put differently, what would be a normative definition of public space? Public space, if it is going to play a role in democratic life, must be a hybrid of actual physical places and active public spheres.[2] To tie public spaces to public spheres we must investigate the constantly changing intersections of physical places, the laws and regulations that govern them, the people who claim them through their use or demands, and the actions of government officials to answer these demands. The cases presented in this book illustrate the tenuous condition of such a normative definition of public space.

Over time, public spaces both become and cease to be public. For example, an atrium manager may post new rules that prohibit otherwise legal activities such as sleeping or loitering. As long as those rules are enforced, that atrium is not a public space. A government building's plaza may be redesigned to make protests and demonstrations impossible or difficult. As long as the redesign remains in place, that plaza is not a public space. The state may condemn an entire neighborhood against the wishes of those who live, work, and own businesses there. So long as their concerns are ignored, that neighborhood is not a public space. This book traces the ways in which spaces become public through the histories of three exterior spaces and three interior spaces in Manhattan. Each story highlights different aspects of the public space–public sphere hybrid.

Given the tendency for corporate interests to usurp public interests in American cities, this hybrid may seem nearly impossible to achieve or maintain.[3] How many public spaces exist? As the cases in this book indicate, perhaps very few do so for very long. While we may be hard-pressed to find a dynamic public space, we can try to map the qualities of particular places and especially the social and political processes that define them against a model of what public space might be. From this overlaid map we may begin to propose ways of rebuilding connections among a place's democratic, social, and physical elements. The goal of this book is to do exactly that: to propose a definition of public space that can inform a critical approach to understanding existing sites, and ultimately to show how such sites may be reactivated as public spaces.

In order to understand public spaces as the sites and subjects of democratic processes, we must ground these concepts in case studies of existing places across stretches of time, and also use a series of methodological lenses: as an economist, to evaluate the distribution of wealth; as a lawyer, to examine the regulations on public spaces as platforms for speech; as a political scientist, to determine who has the authority to make changes to physical places over time; as an environmental and behavioral psychologist, to trace the patterns and habits of sociability that certain spatial configurations might support; and as a public policy researcher, to compare the intentions of public programs with their multivariate effects.

I am none of these. I come to these questions from the discipline of landscape architecture, and I try to map the processes that lead to the development of public spaces and that shape their roles in cities. Designers of the built environment—including landscape architects, architects, and interior, graphic, and urban designers—have a responsibility to understand how their work affects and is affected by the societies they serve. Design researchers can contribute to these efforts by testing, against the actual histories of specific places, what we think the built environment and its production make possible. A vast and growing body of research in fields that include

INTRODUCTION

geography, political science, and art criticism offer entry points and methods to build these understandings.[4]

Design fields tend to define public spaces according to their physical types—parks, plazas, streets, and sidewalks—rather than by their social and political effects. This lack of attentiveness to the politics of public space does not mean that designers view the role of public spaces as unimportant. To the contrary: they view the design of public space as one of the most important contributions of the profession. However, examining the politics of design from within the design fields is fraught with difficulties. It necessitates a comparison of our idea of how public space serves a greater public good with the relation of actual spaces to social, economic, and political inequities. Clients who pay the bills for the development and maintenance of public spaces—city agencies, Business Improvement Districts, and nonprofit parks conservancies, for example—may not want to make their spaces and the processes that govern them open and accessible. But however difficult it may be in practice for designers to challenge their clients, design is crucial to the development and maintenance of dynamic public spaces.

Design is a way of representing ideas, imagining futures, and transforming the built environment. Design shapes physical spaces, creating settings that produce aesthetic experiences for those who move through and occupy them.[5] A designer sets boundaries within a space, connects it to or blocks it from adjacent spaces, lifts it above or pushes it below the street, and creates backdrops of vegetation, polished marble, or advertisements. A designer highlights aspects of a place's history and leaves other aspects hidden. But how do any of these actions relate to questions of the public sphere? And how do design's other roles of representing ideas and imagining futures come to bear?

Existing design-based studies of public space offer some clues, but most do not value public spaces for their ties to public spheres. Constrained by incomplete definitions, the scope and findings of their research are limited. Most scholarship from design fields emphasizes the role of public space as a site for relaxing, recreating, and enjoying everyday social encounters. The goal of many of these studies is to examine spaces that "succeed" in providing settings for such activities and to offer pattern books for practitioners and communities in order to reproduce them in locations. They use case studies to extract successful physical and programmatic qualities so that they can be applied elsewhere; they extract, distill, and apply rather than problematize and question. As a result, such studies do not reflect the ways in which design may produce or preclude dynamic public spaces.

In *How to Turn a Place Around: A Handbook for Creating Successful Public Spaces,* the nonprofit organization Project for Public Spaces (PPS) presents the results of their research on "more than 1,000 public spaces around the world."[6] This approach is limited at the outset by its goal of producing a "handbook for creating successful public spaces" and by its definition of public space, which emphasizes "accessibility, comfort, activities, and sociability"—terms very different from those used in fields like geography and political science that see successful public spaces as sites for conflict and debate. By distilling the physical qualities that the PPS believes support accessibility, activities, comfort, and sociability, the PPS promotes a model for an idealized community where only good things happen; a space apart from the contradictions and problems of American cities. Even a cursory comparison of the PPS's findings with those of researchers in geography and sociology shows the limits of the PPS's research methods. Whereas the PPS values public spaces in New York because they "represent New York in the way the Eiffel Tower represents Paris," "benefit cities economically" by increasing surrounding land values, and offer "free and open forums for people to encounter art,"[7] others argue that such results do not necessarily benefit people who live there. Indeed, applying idealized models of public spaces and neighborhoods can price out existing residents. Christopher Mele's book *Selling the Lower East Side* offers a historic example:

> through the deployment of certain place representations and not others, real estate investment actions and state development policies are presented as compulsory, the subsequent social costs are exculpated, and the resident's resistance and counterclaims to neighborhood changes are also disregarded.[8]

So long as we live in a society in which increases in land value benefit a few landowners and lead to rising rents for everyone else, the PPS's description of this "benefit" to cities remains suspect.[9]

Even if we do acknowledge a role for public space beyond relaxation and recreation, it is difficult to trace the ways in which public spaces relate to immaterial concepts like democracy. *Public Space,* by Stephen Carr, Mark Francis, Leanne G. Rivlin, and Andrew M. Stone, describes the role of public space in public life as providing for "basic human needs" in being "responsive, democratic and meaningful." The authors describe "democratic spaces" as those that "protect the rights of user groups" and are "accessible to all groups and provide for freedom of action." They add that "[u]ltimately, a public space can be changed by public action, because it is owned by all."[10] As it emphasizes public space as a feature of democratic life, *Public Space* argues that public involvement in the initial design process is crucial. The authors do not, however, attend to the complexity of those relationships in specific places. The concepts, therefore, remain abstract. The book focuses on designing settings without interrogating broader questions such as how design shapes the public of a certain space, how public spaces are tied to public spheres, and how actions to limit access to public spaces may be embedded in the aesthetic experience of a place. The cases in *Public Space* remain illustrative. The lack of interrogation raises the question of how case studies might be used to develop richer pictures of public spaces in cities.

Michael Sorkin's book *Starting from Zero* examines the World Trade Center (WTC) site in order to understand the role of design in public space and public life. Sorkin takes apart the planning process, highlighting how private interests shaped the methods of public involvement in decision making to suit their own objectives. Sorkin also proposes design schemes that look beyond the boundaries of the WTC and address issues of uneven development in the city at large. In one of these schemes, Sorkin proposes that development money be spent in locations like the Bronx, Brooklyn, and Queens, areas that have seen much less investment than lower Manhattan. In this way, Sorkin seeks to understand the WTC as a place in need of an active public sphere and as a potential subject for renewed discussions about development across the city.

In *Placemaking: The Art and Practice of Building Communities*, Lynda Schneekloth and Robert Shibley, like Sorkin in *Starting from Zero* and Carr et al. in *Public Spaces*, delineate the relationships between design and democracy and argue for sustained public involvement in decision making about the built environment. Like Sorkin, Schneekloth and Shibley are researchers and practitioners. They define the role of the design professional as "emphasiz(ing) the process of building relationships among public, private, and not-for-profit entities to overcome the fragmentation of official agency."[11] More than any other researchers in design, Shibley and Schneekloth have attempted to create design processes that *produce* public spheres.

These few examples of design-centered research on public space illustrate a range of definitions and approaches—from the PPS's notion of public space as comfortable sites of sociability, to Shibley and Schneekloth's idea of design as constitutive of public spheres. But how do we understand existing places and the ways in which their physical qualities attended by the PPS and Carr and his coauthors relate to the larger democratic processes that Sorkin and Shibley and Schneekloth see as a prerequisite to public space?

The definition of public space that has guided the case studies in this book—that public space is a kind of hybrid of physical spaces and public spheres—is itself a kind of hybrid. It draws from the work of scholars from varied disciplines. It is based on the assumption that physical space is important to democratic public life and emerges from a vast and growing body of literature that seeks to understand exactly how this is so.[12] As much as we might like to envision the Internet or the shopping mall as the "new public realm," these assertions are naïve, if not hostile, to the physical reality of human life and the systematic exclusion of groups and individuals from public space. Homelessness is a constant threat to many people in the United States, where minimum wage in no way approximates a living wage. Without public space as the only guaranteed location for those without access to private space, individual existence itself is threatened. As the following cases show, laws are only one of a number of factors that dictate who is and who is not part of the "public" of public space.[13]

Of course, saying that physical space is necessary to human life does not explain why it is necessary to democratic life. While writers, including art critic Rosalyn Deutsche, have argued that public space is the place where democracy happens, issues of how and why it happens there and under what conditions have received less attention. Scholarship on regulations governing public protests in public spaces offer clues to the connections between public spaces and larger public spheres:

> public space is a place within which political movements can stake
> out the territory that allows them to be seen (and heard) . . . In
> public space—on street corners or in parks, in the streets during
> riots and demonstrations—political organizations can represent
> themselves to a larger population, and through this representation
> give their cries and their demands some force.[14]

The links between public spaces and democracy are more complex than the former being the physical location for the latter. Public spaces are not mere backdrops for democracy. While public spaces can be settings for demonstrations and protest, they must also have concerned publics who formulate positions about that particular place and who demand action from a governing body, and that governing body must respond. In this way public spaces do not need to be the sites of acts of political speech to be tied to democracy. Perhaps more difficultly, they must themselves be the subjects of ongoing democratic processes.[15]

My understanding of the public sphere as a dynamic relationship among publics formed around issues of concern and bodies accountable for addressing these issues is based on the work of Nancy Fraser, in particular her work that challenges and complicates the definition of public sphere laid out by Jürgen Habermas. Fraser argues that there is no "public"; rather, there are multiple publics, and therefore multiple public spheres. Her recent work on transnational public spheres argues that the nation-state is not the only logical accountable body to which publics must formulate their messages: international or even private corporate bodies may be accountable. This fact makes it difficult to identify accountable bodies, formulate messages, and hold them accountable. The cases in this book indicate how, even in one geographic location, identifying the appropriate body is complicated. It is perhaps clearest in a location like City Hall, but what about across larger geographies like Times Square? What about cases where a public space is privately owned but managed by a city agency, as is the case at the Sony Atrium? In many American cities, direct government management of public spaces such as parks, streets, sidewalks, and even neighborhoods is shifting to quasi or private management. Business Improvement Districts, privately owned public spaces, and parks conservancies are just a few examples of this trend; all point to the challenges of mapping and maintaining public space–public sphere hybrids.

The book is divided into two sections. The first section examines a set of exterior public spaces: the front steps of City Hall, Jacob Javits Plaza, and Times Square. The second half examines a set of interior POPS: the former IBM Atrium, Sony Plaza, and Trump Tower. The chapters do not present histories of these places; rather, they take as their points of departure controversies in each site's history. Some controversies were fought in the courts, others in the fields of art or design criticism. They each implicate a different set of issues that either bind or cut the relationships among public spaces and public spheres. Each raises very different questions about what is good and right when it comes to public space: how it should be managed, designed, used, and even debated.

Chapter 1 explores the relationships between public spaces and the right to free speech. Seen within Fraser's concept of the public realm, the act of speech is the point at which public spheres bring their demands to accountable bodies. The symbolic power of the front steps of City Hall gives importance and legitimacy to words that are spoken there. The steps and City Hall Park have been the site of contestation between Mayor Giuliani and nonprofit and labor groups. One week the mayor allowed thousands of Yankees fans to fill the steps and the park for a victory celebration. The next week, for "safety reason," he limited to twenty-five the number of people who could participate in a World AIDS Day press conference on the steps. This chapter reveals the links between the act of speaking and the spatial aspects of public space, links used by government officials to limit access to public forums, and in turn used by members of public spheres to demand access.

At City Hall, legal battles such as those over freedom of speech between Mayor Giuliani and one of his most outspoken critics, Housing Works, revealed the fragility of public spaces as sites for public spheres: even public spaces that appear to be ideal platforms for representing ideas can be shut down through regulation. And access to public spaces is not just limited by regulation. Design and rhetoric are also powerful tools for determining who may act in public spaces and for what purposes. Chapter 2 examines the ongoing design history of Federal Plaza.[16]

Over a ten-year period, Federal Plaza was redesigned twice: as the location for a controversial work of public art, and as a controversial work of landscape architecture. Both projects—Richard Serra's *Tilted Arc* and Martha Schwartz's Jacob Javits Plaza—generated individual maelstroms of debate. This chapter brings those debates together to understand the ways in which design and the processes that lead to redesign are shaped by conflicting values about the role of public space in public life. While art critics Rosalyn Deutsche and Douglas Crimp argued that public officials manipulated public discourse about *Tilted Arc* in order to gain control over a public space, landscape architectural critics almost never mentioned *Tilted Arc* or the issues raised during the eight-year legal battles that preceded its removal from Federal Plaza. When *Tilted Arc* was mentioned in articles on Jacob Javits Plaza, design critics and Schwartz repeated without question government officials' arguments that *Tilted Arc* prevented public use of the plaza and had to be removed. In this way, Schwartz's design and the content of debates over its success gave concrete form to a government agency's implicit and unchallenged definitions of the public of Federal Plaza.

Chapter 3 discusses the redevelopment of Times Square. Design was here part of larger legal and economic processes of urban renewal that delineated and defined appropriate and inappropriate public bodies.[17] Whereas Federal Plaza's redesign processes were under government control, the redesign of Times Square was promoted by an amalgam of public-private interests. The Times Square redevelopment spanned almost thirty years and involved the condemnation and demolition of nearly three city blocks and the transfer of this property from one set of private landowners to another.[18] In order for the New York State Urban Development Corporation (UDC) to use eminent domain and forcibly purchase properties from their owners, it had to prove that the demolition and rebuilding of Times Square was in the public interest. The UDC argued that Times Square was blighted, underdeveloped, and could "infect" the rest of the city with crime and vice. It implied that the current public of Times Square had to be replaced by a safer and more profitable public. None of the lawsuits against the state were successful, and in the midst of economic recession, the demolition began.

Removing the "bad" public from Times Square was only half the process. The new public had to be drawn in. Proving to commercial investors and consumers that Times Square was really clean, safe, and friendly required a massive imaging campaign, which was led by one of the most famous designers of the late twentieth century, Tibor Kalman. Kalman's campaign, when looked at in the context of the larger redevelopment process it was part of, shows that design as a means of representing futures and of representing public bodies can mask processes that sever public spaces and public spheres.

Unlike government plazas, streets, and sidewalks, POPS result from complicated legal arrangements between government agencies and private developers. Because of the complexity of these arrangements, understanding exactly who is accountable for their management and regulation is anything but transparent. In addition, these spaces are often embedded within private buildings, making their role in public life difficult to decipher. How do law, regulation, discourse, and design affect the public lives that happen there? Each of the three case studies in this book explores POPS that are held up by the New York City Planning Department as the best of the program. The question that underlies chapters 4, 5, and 6 is whether or not a privately owned public space can ever be a dynamic site and the subject of public spheres. New York is not alone in developing private partnerships to provide public spaces. Designers and program coordinators have taken the

INTRODUCTION

position that POPS can work if the contracts drawn between cities and corporations are clear and the amenities that corporations provide in these spaces are sufficient. However, as the three case studies show, clear contracts alone cannot guarantee that the resulting plazas and atriums will be dynamic public spaces. Public space can be guaranteed only through ongoing connections to public spheres.

Chapter 4 describes the transformation of the IBM Atrium in Midtown. When the IBM Atrium first opened to the public in 1983, it received glowing reviews from architecture critics, arts organizations, and visitors. It was called "exuberant," "elegant," an "oasis," and "a tree filled conservatory and public living room rolled into one."[19] The Atrium's most admired feature was its twelve stands of towering bright green bamboo, which set it apart from any other interior public space in the city and, arguably, in the country. Nowhere in the contract with IBM did the Planning Department specify that there should be a grove of bamboo trees that canopied the space; however, since the contract between the Department of City Planning and IBM did not require those aspects of the Atrium's design that made it successful, it did not include provisions to protect those qualities in the face of proposed alterations. The story of the Atrium reveals the insufficiency of the legal structure of the Privately Owned Public Space Program to protect well-designed spaces. And more importantly, the story shows that the program has almost no legal provisions for ongoing public participation of those outside government and business in the processes that change these sites. Finally, the Atrium raises the question of whether any of the city's POPS could ever rightly be called public spaces at all.

Sony Plaza, the focus of chapter 5, sits across Fifty-ninth Street from IBM. Of all the POPS in New York, Sony Plaza presents the most intense mix of retail space and public space and includes amenities like air conditioning, movable tables and chairs, and a public museum of technology. The museum, however, is a thinly veiled marketing tool for Sony. One of Sony's most lucrative markets, and by far the largest portion of the summer "public" of this space, is children.[20] Within the plaza, bizarre interactions between BB the Wonderbot[21] and children waiting to enter the "museum," along with the presence of two Sony retail stores, reveal the trade-offs and windfalls of public-private partnerships. While children are targeted as consumers, those who appear to be poor or homeless have allegedly been targeted for removal. The plaza's design was based on the "best practices" of public space development, but its restrictive codes of conduct limit public access, especially those codes of conduct that reflect the broad city campaigns against the homeless. It also highlights the incompatibility of the ideals of public space as a place of repose and passive recreation and as the only location to which *all* people are guaranteed access.

The role of aesthetics is the subject of chapter 6. Trump Tower, a publicly funded building with a lavish appearance, conveys to visitors the sense that they have entered a private realm. Interestingly, design critics have for the most part ignored the building. Perhaps it has been overlooked because it is considered too garish even to begin to criticize. But the building's lavish style points to fundamental problems with design, aesthetics, and dynamic public spaces. The design of Trump Tower makes it seem as if Trump *allows* access to the public, not that access is a public right. The private style of the public spaces of Trump Tower also masks the fact that the enormous profits Trump made from the sale of the building's luxury condominiums and from the rent of the office and retail spaces are built on a complex set of public funding sources. Whereas the story of IBM reveals the institutional lack of provisions for public participation in decision making and the Sony story reveals the casting of the public as either insiders to be courted for consumption or outsiders to be removed, the aesthetic experience of Trump Tower transforms members of a public body into visitors enjoying the hospitality of Trump's private empire.

How have public spaces in New York changed since 9/11? This question is an obvious one given the premise of this book—that physical spaces matter to public life, and vice versa. All of the cases presented in this book were researched and developed between 1999 and 2005: two years before and four years after 9/11. The answer to how public spaces in New York have changed since 9/11 is that they have changed completely and not at all. For example, at Federal Plaza and City Hall, security increased much earlier than 9/11, in response to the bombing of the Oklahoma City Federal Building and the U.S. bombings in 1998 in Afghanistan and Sudan. The ongoing design history of the WTC site indicates that the redevelopment process has been guided by forces set up before 9/11—patterns of ownership and control based on values of property and rent—and that these forces are so intractable that even focused public attention can do little to shift them.

If we look at broad changes to U.S. domestic policies regarding individual rights, then every public space in the country has changed completely. New laws created under the Patriot Act allow the imprisonment of people without charge, making moot the idea of a "right" to public space. From City

Hall to Trump Tower, public space does not exist because parks, plazas, sidewalks, and streets exist. For a space to be a public space, people who talk about it, use it, and reimagine it must tie it to the nonphysical processes that bind it to our public life: to patterns of law, speech, representation, policy, distribution, and economics. Design as a way of considering, representing, and constructing relationships between people and space can play a role in reforging these connections.

INTRODUCTION

# 1 Public Space as Public Sphere
## The Front Steps of New York's City Hall

> The only thing consistent about this policy is that the
> mayor doesn't want critics on what he thinks are his
> steps, but are really the people's steps.
> > —*Norman Siegel, former executive director, New York*
> > *Civil Liberties Union*

> The very reason laws exist in the first place is so
> that people's rights can be protected and that includes
> the right not to be disturbed, agitated, and abused
> by others.
> > —*Rudolph Giuliani, former New York City mayor*

**The front steps of New York's City Hall** appear as an ideal model of a public space: a public property where groups may gather to criticize decisions of elected officials in full view of others. If we imagine Nancy Fraser's idea of the public sphere as the place where members of a public formulate and deliver messages regarding public issues to those officials who should be held accountable, then there can be no more important location for these activities in New York than City Hall's front steps. The design of the steps of City Hall encourages a very particular kind of civic engagement. Press conferences and demonstrations are different from letters, petitions, phone calls, and hearing testimony. They are more akin to theater and performance: visibility is key, making design all the more important.

The steps' design supports this function by providing a physical setting for the nonphysical public sphere. Even in the absence of speech or protest, the steps evoke their function: if a park looks like a field waiting for a soccer team, the steps of a city hall look like a platform waiting for a speech. When viewed as part of an ensemble, with City Hall's facade and the open plaza below, the steps can be seen as a stage, the facade as a dignified backdrop, and the plaza as a place from which to view and comment upon the performance (Figure 1.1). The permanence of the steps' marble surface and the classical references of their architectural detailing convey legitimacy across time. If the interior of a city hall is the place where elected officials debate and develop policies that affect the lives of city residents and where they hear testimony of individuals about these policies, then the exterior of a city hall is where groups and individuals respond to the consequences of these policies: both celebration and dissent, en masse and in full view of those inside the building and of those going about their day on the sidewalks and streets. They are, symbolically and in reality, a threshold between a government and its citizens.

But while the steps appear through design as an ideal melding of public space and public sphere, their contemporary history indicates that this hybrid is, because of its very potency, a fragile construct. Sites like the front steps of City Hall carry a high political charge. They are the perfect location for demonstration and protest, but they are also the perfect location for government-sponsored spectacle. Accommodating both activities is not a simple problem of scheduling; each often acts against the other. A mayor holds events on the front steps that promote her public image, perhaps by welcoming foreign dignitaries or successful athletes. By presenting information critical of her policies, a nonprofit holds events

Figure 1.1. Bird's-eye view of City Hall, New York, c. 1880. Photograph by Charles Pollock, Boston. Library of Congress Prints and Photographs Division, Washington, D.C.

PUBLIC SPACE AS PUBLIC SPHERE

on the front steps to challenge the mayor's public image. Because the distance between two such kinds of actions—promoting government officials and protesting government decisions—is often so great, and because challenges to a government official's image are often perceived as a threat, officials set out restrictive policies to impede their critics' actions. Through these policies even the best-designed public spaces can cease to serve the purposes of a public sphere.

By examining a series of legal cases regarding front steps of City Hall as a site for free speech, this chapter attempts to map the limits of government-owned public spaces as sites for democratic action. Between 1998 and 2005, Housing Works, a nonprofit organization and outspoken critic of former Mayor Giuliani's politics toward homeless people suffering from HIV/AIDS, fought in court for their right to deliver their message from the steps. The mayor's office sought to block their efforts and eventually to punish them for their messages. While Giuliani's post-9/11 image was that of "America's Mayor," for much of his time in office Giuliani was criticized for not dealing with issues like diminishing units of affordable housing and increasing numbers of people in poverty. The Housing Works story shows that maintaining public space–public sphere hybrids requires ongoing litigation, particularly in locations as central to public life as City Hall.

## The Public Life of City Hall

The importance of the front steps of City Hall as a public space in New York City cannot be underestimated. Over the past two centuries, the steps have been the physical setting for press conferences, demonstrations, the celebration of military victories, the mourning of soldiers and heads of state, and other less overtly political events like mini circuses with real elephants, exhibition boxing matches, and send-offs for city choruses set to travel abroad.

New York's City Hall[1] sits in the southern portion of Manhattan. Its design was the result of a competition won by John McComb Jr. and Joseph Mangin.[2] At the time of its construction between 1803 and 1812, City Hall marked the northern reaches of the city. If the edges of the island of Manhattan reached out into the rivers in a riddled mass of piers and marshes and boats, City Hall marked the northern boundary, turning its best face to the city. The building is part of a complex consisting of the building, a forecourt, and a park, all of which were carefully bound by neatly wrought iron fencing. The front of the building (the south side) was clad in marble at great

**3**

expense. The north side was clad in brownstone to save money. This choice of brownstone would not have detracted from the grandeur of the building, since the north side was thought to be "safely out of site."[3]

A photo of City Hall from 1835 shows the building and its large fenced park flanked by a wide sidewalk. The building's design is straightforward: the main facade includes broad stairs topped with a portico, an additional story and gallery, and a belvedere topped with a copper dome. Two identical wings that extend to the south flank the central portion of the building, creating a shallow courtyard around the steps. The wings give a sense of solidness to the overall structure, anchoring it to its site. The facade also conveys solidness. The regularity of the windows and the orderliness of the columns appear reasoned. The building is not laden with ornament but appears almost regal, particularly in comparison with the places where most New Yorkers of the time spent their days.

The interior of the building is no less impressive. Beyond the lobby is the rotunda, with a grand circular staircase capped by a glass-domed skylight that is supported by ten Corinthian columns. The walls are decorated with 120 portraits of statesmen, former mayors, and military heroes. Figures from the War of 1812 are well represented; this war produced "a new hero daily," and at the time City Hall needed portraits.[4] Also included in the portrait collection are Thomas Jefferson and a number of former city mayors, including John Lindsay, Edward Koch, and David Dinkins.[5]

Photos from the Municipal Archives of the city of New York, the City Hall Library, and newspaper articles illustrate nearly 200 years of spectacles, protests, press conferences, and demonstrations on the front steps of City Hall and in City Hall Park. One of the most elaborate events was the spectacle following the death of President Abraham Lincoln. Though New York residents rejected Abraham Lincoln by a two-to-one margin in the 1864 election, they "embraced him"[6] after his assassination. Descriptions give a sense of the sheer scale of the event:

> A procession of 160,000 people led the hearse, pulled by 16 gray
> horses, to City Hall. For three days, the city literally shut down as
> hundreds of thousands of people poured into its streets, most of
> them content to get a glimpse of the president's hearse and coffin,
> as the viewing of the man himself was almost beyond possibility.[7]

The building was adorned with black streamers and a banner that read "The Nation Mourns" (Figure 1.2). A 1915 report by the American Scenic and

PUBLIC SPACE AS PUBLIC SPHERE

Historic Preservation Society detailed the honoring of the dead sailors from the Vera Cruz at City Hall,[8] saying that the location for the event was

> a natural and instinctive expression of the place which the City Hall holds in the public mind . . . here is focused the sentiment of five and a half million people . . . here they have come to celebrate their military triumphs, civic achievements and great anniversaries.[9]

In 1952 the steps became a replica of the prow of the Flying Enterprise, festooned with red, white, and blue bunting to welcome the "intrepid skipper" who refused to abandon his freighter as it sank in the North Atlantic (Figure 1.3).[10] The Danish skipper who had attracted worldwide attention for his tenacity was received in New York by Mayor Impellitteri and was given the Medal of Honor of the city of New York.[11] In 1981 hundreds of thousands of people greeted the freed American hostages who returned from Iran during a procession from the Battery to City Hall.[12] In 1984 the steps and plaza were used for an amateur heavy-weight exhibition boxing match and an awards ceremony

Figure 1.2. President Lincoln's funeral: removal of the body from City Hall to the funeral car, New York. *Harper's Weekly,* May 13, 1865.

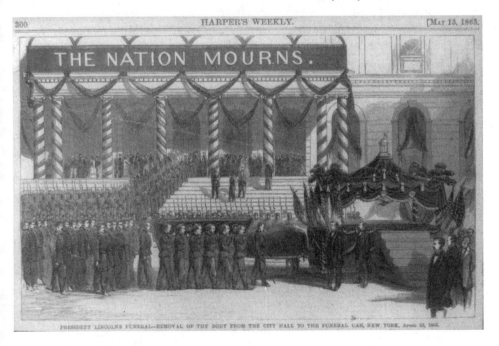

PUBLIC SPACE AS PUBLIC SPHERE

Figure 1.3. The front steps of City Hall transformed into a replica of the bow of *Flying Enterprise*, 1952. Courtesy of NYC Municipal Archives.

for the Joe Louis Memorial Scholarship, and a "grand send-off for athletes en route to the U.S. Youth Games."[13] The steps are the symbolic entrance and exit to the city, where worthies are welcomed and representatives are anointed before representing the city on their voyages. The worthies also "give" something to the iconic history of City Hall and to the current government: a little of their luster rubs off.

A more recent photograph of City Hall offers an entry point into the relationships between public forums, public spaces, and law (Figure 1.4). The photo shows twenty-five people standing on each of the eleven steps of City Hall in rows four abreast. Each person holds a sheet of bluish green 11 × 17–inch paper printed with a number in giant type. No other signs, buttons, or banners are visible: just the numbers 1 through 25. The plaza in front of them is empty except for a security person and a truck. The group takes up about one-sixteenth of the expanse of steps; they look small against the backdrop of the building. If you hold the 4 × 6–inch photo in your hand, you could easily and completely cover the group with your thumb and still be left with an uninterrupted view of the steps and the building. The date stamped on the back of the print is July 16, 1998.

PUBLIC SPACE AS PUBLIC SPHERE

What appears to be a photograph of the most enigmatic protest ever held is actually a piece of evidence produced by the New York Civil Liberties Union (NYCLU) for their client, Housing Works. As an image it is puzzling. As a piece of evidence it is rather brilliant. The photo illustrates one of the NYCLU's main arguments: that Mayor Giuliani and Police Department Commissioner Howard Safir denied Housing Works the opportunity to speak from the steps by making false claims about how many people could safely gather there.

## Law, Speech, and Public Space

Before examining the Housing Works cases, it is important to discuss the relationships between public spaces and the right to free speech. Examining controls on speech in public spaces and challenges to these controls requires a combination of spatial, historical, policy, and legal analysis. While there is no legal definition of public space, there are three points of law governing free speech that also set out basic relationships between speech and space.

First, public spaces such as streets, sidewalks, and parks have, relative to the First Amendment, special status as traditional public forums

Figure 1.4. City Hall, New York, July 16, 1998. New York Civil Liberties Union.

where one's right to speak is guaranteed. The court case that describes traditional public forums is *Hague v. Committee for Industrial Organization* 307 U.S. 496 (1939). Hague sets out streets and parks as a central part of civic life

> (w)herever the title of streets and parks may rest, they have
> immemorially been held in trust for the use of the public and,
> time out of mind, have been used for purposes of assembly,
> communicating thoughts between citizens, and discussing public
> questions. Such use of the streets and public places has, from
> ancient times, been a part of the privileges, immunities, rights,
> and liberties of citizens.

It is important to note that Hague does not refer specifically to *public spaces,* rather to a set of landscape types that are typically thought of as types of public spaces: streets, parks, and public *places.* Hague deems traditional public forums as fundamental to democracy.

Second, while speech in traditional public forums is a protected activity, it is also a regulated activity. In the same paragraph in which Hague discusses traditional public forums and the right to speak there, he goes on to argue that even in these places speech may be regulated:

> The privilege of a citizen of the United States to use the streets
> and parks for communication of views on national questions may
> be regulated in the interest of all; it is not absolute, but relative,
> and must be exercised in subordination to the general comfort
> and convenience, and in consonance with peace and good order;
> but it must not, in the guise of regulation, be abridged or denied.

Put differently, while the content of speech cannot be regulated in public forums, the time, location, and manner of the act of speech can be regulated. Hague acknowledges that regulation of speech can be used to suppress speech, particularly by "Directors of Safety."[14] As Don Mitchell has argued, controls on time, place, and manner are much more effective than outright censorship. They are harder to argue against. They are complicated to sniff out. We are so attached to the idea of decorum that we have in some ways accepted peace and quiet as substitutes for social justice. We are so attached to freedom of speech as simply the freedom to say what you want that we have forgotten that speech must have an audience—the right audience—to be effective.

8

Different locations within a city are more or less "charged"; that is, buildings like City Hall and main thoroughfares like Broadway carry more representational weight than the sidewalks around their perimeters. Events that take place in such locations appear to be more mainstream than events that take place in "marginal" locations. Depending on the time of an event, there will be significantly more onlookers. Controlling the time also controls the duration of an event. An all-night vigil during which participants "sleep" on sidewalks presents a powerful message regarding homelessness. The steps of City Hall are politically charged because of their proximity to seats of government, their history as important sites of representation, and their visually symbolic designs. In the realm of the civic geography of New York City, City Hall remains *the* location for important public messages. It is both the actual place where decisions are made and the symbolic heart of the city. The steps are a kind of liminal space between the inside of the building and the outside—or the larger city itself. Conflicts over speech in such places are inevitable.

Third, any rules set up governing traditional public forums must "(1) be content neutral, (2) be narrowly tailored to meet a significant government interest, and (3) leave open ample alternative means for communication."[15] Proving that rules set out to govern a traditional public forum are content neutral involves proving that all groups who try to speak from a particular location have been subject to the same regulations regardless of the content of their message. Proving that rules are narrowly tailored involves an analysis of why certain rules are enacted. Most often rules are created to address issues of safety and security. Proving that there are alternative sites available for speech acts can be interpreted to mean that an alternative site has the same political potency as the original. Arguably, there is no alternative site for speaking out against city policy than from the front of City Hall itself.

Housing Works' legal battles over the steps of City Hall show how government agencies use the time, location, and manner doctrine to limit the speech acts of groups with which they disagree. Using the authority afforded them by the doctrine, the mayor and police commissioner blocked, shrank, and pushed off to the side Housing Works' press conferences. While the front steps of a city hall do not fall under Hague's category of streets, sidewalks, and parks, the more than 200 years of use of the steps as a public forum shows their vital importance as a platform for speech: both for messages from City Hall to New Yorkers and for messages from New Yorkers to City Hall. Giuliani held events on the steps to bolster his public image.

Housing Works sought to use the same location to tie the suffering caused by Giuliani's policies directly to the mayor—to shift his image from representative of the public body to that of a criminal responsible for the death of thousands of New Yorkers.

## Housing Works' Fight for the Steps

The battles over the front steps of City Hall between Mayor Giuliani[16] and Housing Works took place over four years.[17] The story of the conflicts between Housing Works and the city indicates that regulations on speech can be used repeatedly to block unwanted messages and, therefore, challenges to controls on speech must be persistent and ongoing. It shows the vulnerability of public forums to controls, but also indicates ways in which speech can be defended in public forums. Since the Housing Works cases involved more than one incident, we can see how the mayor's office and the police commissioner responded to a group's ongoing policy challenges. It was not a one-time denial of access based on a particular reason; rather, the administration tweaked its policies and enforcement patterns in response to legal challenges and, almost without exception, the way they tweaked these policies related to spatial controls on the speech—that is, they regulated how bodies were allowed to occupy the space. By limiting the number of people engaged in the speech activity, the administration sought to diminish the perceived strength and importance of the message. Each change they made to regulations further tested the limits of the use of spatial controls on speech and the degree to which a place's design—its size and configuration—was able to support acts of speech.

A parallel set of events on the steps of City Hall that took place during the time of the Housing Works lawsuits emphasizes the importance of the steps as a site of representation for the mayor himself. During his tenure as mayor, Giuliani, like mayors before him, used the steps and the facade of City Hall as a backdrop for the construction of his public image—an image frequently at odds with his own policies and declarations about what constitutes good citizenship and good leadership. Giuliani was a mayor many New Yorkers loved to hate. Animosity toward the mayor came from many camps, including nonprofits angered by his cuts to social services such as Housing Works, and also from city workers, including police, teachers, nurses, and construction and sanitation workers, who faced wage freezes during a time of budget surpluses.

PUBLIC SPACE AS PUBLIC SPHERE

The criticisms that Housing Works launched against the mayor were more damning than those of city workers, and Giuliani's desire to separate Housing Works' message from his image was arguably more acute. Housing Works argued that the mayor's cuts to funding for people with AIDS fueled the spread of the disease and sped the deaths of those who suffered from it. While signs at a teacher's rally against wage freezes read "Hey Rudy, Shake Your Booty," and demanded increased funding for schools and teachers (Figure 1.5), signs at a Housing Works press conference featured signs of Giuliani's face stamped with the label "AIDS Criminal" in red ink.[18]

It is not surprising that Giuliani would prefer this "AIDS Criminal" image not be broadcast in front of his offices. In fact, Giuliani viewed *not being* "disturbed, harassed or abused" by others as a *right* that should be protected by the law. In a 1996 speech titled "The Next Phase of Quality of Life: Creating a More Civil City," Giuliani berated the "cynics" of his programs and policies.[19] (We can imagine that Housing Works falls into this category of "cynics." Giuliani stated that "optimism" promoted "quality of life.") He also argued that focusing energy and resources on punishing people who diminished "quality of life"[20] would prevent "more serious antisocial behavior." Giuliani pledged to work to make people act in a dignified way toward each other, because "inconsiderate behavior leads to disorder." For example, he argued that while graffiti and murder are "vastly different crimes," they were

Figure 1.5. Demonstration on sidewalk outside City Hall fence, 1996.

PUBLIC SPACE AS PUBLIC SPHERE

nonetheless part of the "same continuum." With such a warped sense of what constitutes a right and what constitutes a violation of a right, it should be unsurprising that Giuliani frequently found himself in court. Many groups and individuals found reason to be cynical of Giuliani's policies and sought to deliver their message with City Hall as their backdrop. The NYCLU participated in thirty-three First Amendment cases against the mayor, prevailing either entirely or in part in twenty-four of those cases.[21] Several cases were filed on behalf of Housing Works beginning in July 1998 and extending after Giuliani's term in office ended in 2001.

In July 1998, the police department rejected a request by Housing Works to hold a press conference on the steps of City Hall. Housing Works planned the event to coincide with the first anniversary of the 1997 passage of Local Law 49, which created the New York City Division of AIDS Services and which required that the city provide certain services to New Yorkers afflicted with AIDS and HIV. During the press conference, Housing Works intended to release a new report that "documented the City's failure to provide these services."[22] Charles King, co–executive director of Housing Works, said that his group wanted to use the City Hall site because "that was where Mr. Giuliani signed a law one year ago that was designed to improve services to people with AIDS."[23] Housing Works stated that the event would last an hour or less and would involve up to fifty people.

The police department denied Housing Works' request, citing an April 1994 memorandum that limited the number of people who could be present at such events to twenty-five people for reasons of "safety and security."[24] The NYCLU argued that this policy was not uniformly enforced. They noted that between January 1, 1995, and July 1998, there were at least fifty-three city-sponsored events that occurred directly in front of City Hall and that most of these events involved more than fifty people.[25] For example, in May 1998, to celebrate New York Yankees pitcher David Wells's perfect game, the mayor held a rally involving about 300 people.[26] On October 29, 1996, thousands of New Yorkers gathered at a City Hall–sponsored celebration of the New York Yankees' World Series victory, at which the mayor issued a proclamation naming the day "New York Yankees Day."[27] This particular celebration at City Hall was preceded by what was considered by many to have been the biggest sports parade in the city's history. Giuliani himself announced that more than 3.5 million people came out for the parade. This estimate may have been "based more on civic pride than reality," according to the *Toronto Star*,[28] and "could have been accommodated only if quite a few

PUBLIC SPACE AS PUBLIC SPHERE

fans were lying crushed underfoot," according to the *New York Times*.[29] However, photographs of the event at City Hall showed the steps packed with people, including the mayor, the Rockettes, the Yankees, and fans. The plaza in front of the steps was also filled (Figure 1.6).[30]

In his opinion, Judge Baer stated that the city appeared to have "unbridled discretion to grant exceptions" and could arguably "grant exceptions to those groups whose speech it agrees with and deny exceptions to those groups whose speech it disagrees with." Baer noted the importance of the site in the geography of civic places in New York, and stated that the steps have "a symbolic importance that City Hall Park does not." Baer made specific reference to the NYCLU photos of the group of twenty-five on the steps, stating that that group demonstrated "beyond peradventure" that the front steps of City Hall were so large that groups greater than twenty-five would not cause "significant congestion," and would "allow for ample ingress and egress." Put differently, the steps, because of their design, were well suited to acts of speech involving groups of people. Baer also added that when compared with the population of New York, "a group of 25 people does not even begin to provide a fair cross-section of those in our community who are likely to be interested in attending and participating in a particular press conference." Baer granted Housing Works a preliminary injunction against the city, and the city was ordered to allow the event to take place with

Figure 1.6. Yankees victory celebration at City Hall, 1996. Archives of Rudolph Giuliani.

fewer than fifty people.[31] Housing Works held their event on July 22, 1998, without incident.

The evidence presented in this case shows that the mayor and the police commissioner did indeed selectively enforce controls on speech activities based on the content of the speech. Prior to Housing Works' request for the press conference, the organization had already been an outspoken critic of the mayor's health policies. The mayor had every reason to expect that Housing Works' press conference and report would publicly tie him to the deaths of New Yorkers made homeless at a time of great physical and, one can imagine, great emotional vulnerability.

Baer's opinion highlights the way in which the police commissioner and the mayor used safety and security as screens for controlling the content of messages delivered from the steps. He also argued that limiting groups to twenty-five people was unfounded when compared to the actual capacity of the steps and that such a limited number of individuals could not adequately represent a concerned community. Put differently, the physical scale of the protest would be insufficient to symbolically represent the actual number of people affected by a city-wide policy. It is important to note that Giuliani and Safir did not deny Housing Works access entirely, but rather sought to lessen the impact of their event by reducing the number of participants. Events with large numbers of people indicate broad support. Those with few people, particularly against a backdrop the size of City Hall, appear to have little support. By extension, the issues themselves seem less important. When it comes to speech, size matters. Limits on the number of participants are also limits on the perceived legitimacy of the message itself.

During 1998 and 1999, the mayor and the police commissioner continued to rewrite and selectively enforce policies regarding press conferences on the steps of City Hall, and Housing Works continued to challenge their actions in the courts. In late August 1998, New York City officials tightened security around City Hall in response to the United States' bombing targets in Sudan and Afghanistan. Concrete barricades were positioned around the building and police cars were used to block access to the parking lot. Only those people who could prove they had business in City Hall were allowed through the barricade. In August or September 1998 the city adopted a new policy banning all events from the steps of City Hall. While security seems an incontestable concern, how does one weigh it against concerns regarding the closure of an important public forum, arguably the most important public forum in New York? This question proved to be irrelevant in light of

**14**

PUBLIC SPACE AS PUBLIC SPHERE

the mayor's subsequent actions and his seemingly cavalier attitude toward safety and security on the steps. In October 1998,[32] Mayor Giuliani and Police Commissioner Howard Safir gave permission for a victory celebration for the New York Yankees. The mayor wore a Yankees jacket and cap and waved to the crowds from the center of the float as it traveled down the Canyon of Heroes to a ceremony at City Hall.[33] During the celebration, the police permitted between 5,000 and 6,000 people to occupy the steps. The event took place over the course of a day, from about 9:00 AM to 3:00 PM.[34]

Clearly, celebrating the Yankees' victory and linking the Yankees' elevated status to City Hall and to Mayor Giuliani's career was more important than protecting City Hall from possible terrorist activities or than ensuring safe evacuation routes in case of an emergency. Yet, less than one month after the celebration, the mayor and police commissioner played the safety-and-security card again when they refused to allow Housing Works to hold an event on December 1 "at or near the steps of City Hall" to commemorate World AIDS Day. In an attempt to protect the city from litigation regarding its refusal to allow the event, the city immediately drew up a new policy to govern the use of the steps.[35] The policy was clearly self-serving. It protected events that bolstered the image of the mayor, and gave great powers to the executive branch of city government to decide what happens on the steps and when. The new policy prohibited all events from taking place on the steps with the following exceptions:

> The Police Commissioner may authorize the use by the City of
> the City Hall plaza and step areas for ceremonial occasions (1) of
> extraordinary public interest, (2) which are uniquely appropriate
> to City Hall, (3) during which the regular business of City Hall
> may be suspended or curtailed and City Hall otherwise closed to
> the general public, (4) which are unique, non-annual events of
> major civic and City-wide importance (e.g. inaugurations and
> events honoring national military triumphs, space exploration,
> extraordinary national or world leaders or local World
> Championship teams), and (5) which require a ticket for entry,
> provided the Police Commissioner or his designee determines
> that adequate provisions for security can be made in light of the
> extraordinary security concerns outlined above.[36]

While the policy's reference to "space exploration" might seem odd, it made sense in light of the fact that a week after the day the policy was written the city held, for John Glenn and other crew members of the space shuttle *Discovery*, a parade down the Canyon of Heroes and a large ceremony on the steps of City Hall. The city distributed about 3,000 tickets for the event, and people who attended had similar access to the steps of City Hall as did those who attended the Yankees' celebration the month before.[37]

Housing Works and the NYCLU applied again for an injunction through the courts, this time seeking permission to hold their World AIDS Day event. The injunction was granted on November 24, 1998.[38] Housing Works held their press conference on December first; however, within the geography of City Hall, Housing Works and their message were pushed to the margins. Housing Works was not allowed access to the steps at all. Instead, the police department required them to hold their event in a parking lot. The police department also used metal barricades to make an enclosure for a speaker's area that could hold about fifty people, and a separate enclosure for about 200 people participating in the rally and demonstration. Police required participants to stay in their "pens."[39]

Over the next six months, the city repeatedly violated its own policy by allowing four press conferences to take place on the steps. The NYPD was present at all of these events and did not prevent the events from taking place even though they violated policy. No barricades were used at any of the press conferences.

A similar set of events unfolded in 1999. The mayor made adjustments to his policy regarding the steps, and the police commissioner enforced the policy unevenly. Housing Works continued to be treated exceptionally, and responded to this treatment via legal avenues. The mayor in turn made minor adjustments to the policy. For example, in February 1999 Housing Works filed for summary judgment based on the grounds that the policy was unconstitutional.[40] Two days after Housing Works filed for summary judgment, the city amended their November policy, making the following additions: everyone entering the City Hall area should be subject to search, events taking place in the plaza area should be limited to fifty people, and members of the City Council can hold events on the steps of City Hall as long as there are no more than fifty people.[41] They added that if there were a specific security threat "City Hall steps and plaza area may be subject to additional restrictions or closure."[42] Under this policy, no events could take place on the steps unless either the mayor or a member of the City Council sponsored the event; in other words, unless the message were sanctioned by someone inside City Hall.[43]

**16**

On Tuesday, March 16, 1999, the NYCLU informed the city that Housing Works intended to hold a press conference and demonstration at City Hall and that the event was not sponsored by a member of the City Council. The NYPD stated it would not allow the event to take place on the steps of City Hall. The rally and press conference were held March 23, and criticized Mayor Giuliani's policies regarding AIDS policies. The NYPD required Housing Works to hold their event in the part of the City Hall parking lot that was farthest away from City Hall itself. They were also surrounded by metal barricades.[44]

One week after the press conference and rally, Housing Works informed the city that it intended to file a summary judgment motion against the amended policy because it stipulated that only events sponsored by a member of the City Council could be held on the front steps of City Hall.[45] The city suspended the policy for ninety days. Events that were not sponsored by a member of the City Council but were deemed by the mayor to be of "extraordinary public interest" were allowed to take place on the steps. However, those that were not deemed by the mayor as such were limited to fifty people and could last for no more than one hour. During this ninety-day period, many press conferences took place on the steps with "no incident."[46]

In June 1999 the city informed the court of their new rules regarding events at or near the steps of City Hall, limiting the number of people who could attend an event there to fifty:

> excluding public ceremonies and commemorations,
> inaugurations, award ceremonies, celebrations, festivals, and
> similar events that have traditionally been organized or sponsored
> by the City of New York and administered by the Department of
> Citywide Administrative Services and/or the Department of Parks
> and Recreation.[47]

Housing Works planned an event for late September 1999 at which it was set to release a new report that described the city's failure to conform to a law that required the city to provide housing to individuals with AIDS. Housing Works also planned to have clients of the Division of AIDS Services speak out at the demonstration. Housing Works argued that the location of the demonstration was important. It wanted clients to have the opportunity to "symbolically directly tell the Mayor of the impact of his failure to implement the law on their lives."[48] Charles King added:

we feel that this is very specifically, this administration and more specifically the Mayor's duty to ensure that the law is properly carried out and that the Mayor has made a deliberate decision not to implement the law, and so we want to come to him directly and point this failure out to him in a very public way. At the same time, we want to catch the attention of the City Council that is also housed in City Hall. They enacted this law very specifically because the Giuliani administration had proposed the elimination of the Division of AIDS Services and the elimination of services that the division was providing at the time. So they enacted the law to force the administration to continue to provide those services and to provide them adequately, and we want the City Council to know that the Mayor isn't doing that.[49]

Mr. King argued that by limiting the size of the press conference, the mayor was effectively controlling how the event would be perceived publicly: "Obviously, the fewer people you can muster to come out for an event, the less seriously the event is treated by the press, the less seriously it is treated by the administration and other targeted audiences."[50] Consistent with this concern, Mr. King testified that the mayor was quoted in the papers gloating that only 250 people attended the December 1, 1998, World AIDS Day event.[51] Defending the city's use of enclosures for relatively small crowds, the mayor quipped, "(w)e can't help it if these people exaggerate their turnout."[52] Not only did the mayor's strategy of marginalizing and shrinking Housing Works' press conference work, but the mayor also represented the Housing Works event to the press as if the reason the turnout was so low was because the organization did not have the support base it purported.

When Housing Works took Giuliani and Safir to court, the NYCLU presented three ways in which the policy was unconstitutional. First, judging events as either of "extraordinary public interest" or not, it "explicitly and impermissibly" allowed differential treatment of speakers based on the content of their speech. It was not just that the mayor decided what was or was not of "extraordinary public interest" but that he judged the content of the speech and treated speakers differently based on that content. Housing Works also argued that the policy was unconstitutional because it had no "specific, objective and definite standards required of licensing schemes."[53] It argued finally that the limit of events to only fifty people was not "narrowly tailored to the defendants' legitimate interests," or, in other words, the policy did not give specific and legitimate reasons for this number. The NYCLU anticipated that the city would argue that the legitimate interest of having only fifty was security-related (this lawsuit took place before 9/11 but after the Oklahoma City bombings). However, the NYCLU argued that the city had stated that "[n]either the NYPD nor the FBI has received any information suggesting that City Hall specifically is the intended target of any terrorist activity." They also noted that the city already required all those participating in protests at City Hall to pass through metal detectors and advised protesters that they may have their bags searched. They added:

> [t]he plaintiff fully recognizes that there are dangers in the world
> that justify unusual measures in some circumstances but
> respectfully submits that one of the greatest dangers in a
> democratic society such as ours occurs when the government
> uses undifferentiated allegations of security and "terrorism" to
> suppress the rights of peaceful assembly and protest. That is what
> the City is doing in this case, and the First Amendment does not
> permit that.[54]

The judge ruled in favor of Housing Works.[55]

While it is beyond the scope of this chapter to discuss all the cases filed against Giuliani by Housing Works,[56] the most recent case, decided in May 2005, marks not only the end of the litigation against the former mayor but also shows the extent to which Giuliani was willing to go not only to block or weaken Housing Works' messages but also to weaken the organization itself. The case found that beginning in 1997, Giuliani punished Housing Works for criticism of himself, his aides, and his policies by cutting Housing Works' government contracts to provide housing and services to people with HIV/AIDS.[57] As a result of the May 2005 ruling, Housing Works is to receive $4.8 million in damages, lawyers' fees, and interest.

The Housing Works cases show that public officials can control speech in public spaces—even in those spaces whose designs appear ideally suited to such activities. However, the cases also point to methods for maintaining public spaces as dynamic and vital sites for democratic action. An understanding of the former is necessary for the latter. While the right to speak in a public space is not absolute, neither are the regulations or enforcement attempts by elected officials or police. The courts are crucial sites in these ongoing processes. But cases can be fought only in response to the enforcement of regulation. Unless regulation restricting speech in public spaces is constantly tested, it will remain. Those seeking to protect their right to speak

PUBLIC SPACE AS PUBLIC SPHERE

in public forums must keep record of shifting policies and the unevenness of enforcement of those policies. They must also have access to legal representation and be ready to spend a great deal of time in court.

Understanding the law, monitoring its enforcement, testing it by engaging in speech acts, and litigating to ensure access—this is the process by which public spaces are protected as sites for public spheres. Each step in the process is dependant on the other steps. Without this process, there is no necessary connection between democratic action and public space. This process is costly. For Housing Works, these costs came as staff time and lawyers fees and as the (temporary) suspension of government contracts. Housing Works could have used these resources to better serve their clients. The NYCLU also spent resources that might have funded other projects.

But the near-constant litigation cost Giuliani very little. He is no longer mayor. The city will be forced to pay the settlement, not Giuliani personally. Faced with the opportunity of punishing a stalwart critic at little personal risk, Giuliani chose to limit Housing Works' access to City Hall and he turned a blind eye when one of his appointees further punished the organization by cutting their city contracts. In doing so, he sought to silence an organization and indirectly to silence all the people on whose behalf the organization spoke: the most vulnerable New Yorkers, those who were dying and had no place to live, who suffered as a result of Giuliani's cuts to public programs and had no place in the image of the city Giuliani was manufacturing—an image directly tied to his own personal image. Giuliani made room on the steps only for healthy, uncritical, or profitable bodies, opening the Canyon of Heroes and welcoming them to wave with him from New York's civic heart.

The photo of the twenty-five people on the steps of City Hall captures one moment in an ongoing battle. It demonstrates the illegality of the enforcement of limits on how many people can speak from this public platform. Speech acts in public spaces challenge efforts to limit who can speak, maintaining the vibrancy of public forums. But the image also reminds us that the public is not a uniform entity. Controls on who speaks in public forums are also controls on who *appears* as part of the public. Housing Works' message was twofold: that people who have HIV/AIDS and are homeless are part of New York's public, and, as Sander Gilman has argued, that representations of those suffering from HIV/AIDS "mark the function and place of the sufferer in relation to the society in which he or she dwells."[58] People with HIV/AIDS are subject to societal fantasies used to "create a boundary between ourselves and the afflicted . . . to distance and isolate those we designate as ill."[59] By cutting funding to provide people with HIV/AIDS access to private spaces of the home and by actively thwarting their attempts to appear in public, it could be argued that Giuliani sought their double erasure.[60] It also reminds us that public spaces and private spaces are linked: in this case, through public policy.

At the World AIDS Day vigil on December 1, 2004, in City Hall Park, volunteers read the names of the more than 80,000 known to have died from AIDS in New York City.[61] The reading took place over a twenty-four-hour period that began at midnight. Volunteers took turns speaking from four platforms set up in a semicircle (Figure 1.7). One volunteer read the names in sign language. As each name was announced, statistics were transformed into individuals who were each remembered twice: once by the reader and once by the listener. Each name was heard for a brief moment. The event was not a permanent memorial.

The Smithsonian National Museum of American History includes in their 9/11 collection items of clothing that belonged to Mayor Giuliani: the boots he wore to the site, a baseball cap, and two jackets. His boots are captioned "The mayor's leadership helped New York City recover and rebuild."[62] Giuliani's work in the months following the attacks was exemplary. But perhaps the Smithsonian should cross-reference this exhibit with Giuliani's efforts to

Figure 1.7. World AIDS Day Vigil in City Hall Park, December 1, 2003.

thwart the First Amendment at City Hall and with the $4.8 million bill he left for New Yorkers to pay.[63]

The next chapter examines Federal Plaza, a government-owned space tied to an important government building, and officials' attempts to control what happens there and therefore who its public is. But unlike the case of the steps at City Hall, at Federal Plaza, regulation was not the tool of choice. Instead, officials used design.

# 2 Art or Lunch? Redesigning a Public for Federal Plaza

*This is a day for the people to rejoice ... because now the plaza returns rightfully to the people.*
    —*William Diamond, New York regional administrator*
    *for the General Services Administration*

**At City Hall,** legal battles over freedom of speech and assembly showed that even places that seem intended to be locations for acts of protest can be controlled through regulation. Regulation changes the symbolic and real possibility of places even when the places themselves remain physically unaltered. Ties between the steps of City Hall and the activities of the public sphere were severed and then reestablished through ongoing processes of regulation, speech acts, and litigation. Throughout this process, the steps themselves never physically changed. The story of 26 Federal Plaza offers no such physical constant. The plaza was redesigned twice in the space of ten years. Motivating each redesign were specific ideas about what public life should be. Each redesign framed particular publics by creating particular spatial and aesthetic settings.

While studying places that have been altered dramatically in a short space of time makes unraveling the values surrounding these changes difficult, it also affords us the opportunity to examine in greater detail the ways in which design—as a process of decision making and as a physical product—and the rhetoric of critique and debate surrounding design generate ideas about public space and its position as the site and subject of active public spheres. For example, contracts between government agencies, artists, and designers spell out the form and function of public plazas; a plaza's form and function make certain kinds of activities there possible while making other activities difficult or impossible; design critics find fault with or praise new public spaces; implicit or explicit attempts to make physical changes to a plaza result in public hearings; hearing testimony reveals competing definitions of the role of public space and public art; and new government design contracts generate new physical settings and new rounds of conflicts.[1]

The history of Federal Plaza/Jacob Javits Plaza shows how government officials, artists, designers, and critics engage in ongoing processes of design, critique, and redesign. These processes define and redefine public space and public life. In 1979 artist Richard Serra physically changed the plaza by installing his sculpture *Tilted Arc*. He created *Tilted Arc* based on the idea that public art on a government-owned site should be confrontational and never complicit. Government officials did not share Serra's values. They viewed the sculpture as an eyesore and a threat, and they actively and successfully sought to have the sculpture removed. The values of the government officials were not shared by art critics Rosalyn Deutsche and Douglas Crimp, who viewed Federal Plaza without Serra's sculpture as emblematic of what public space and public life should *not* be: actively controlled by a few powerful and determined people. The values of the art critics were not shared by landscape architect Martha Schwartz, who redesigned Federal Plaza in accordance with the wishes of the government agency that hired her. At this time, the plaza was renamed Jacob Javits Plaza. Design critic Clare Cooper-Marcus did not share Schwartz's view of how a public space should be designed, and has condemned the plaza.

This is of course a simplification of the story. Serra's *Tilted Arc* and Schwartz's Jacob Javits Plaza generated individual maelstroms of critique and countercritique about what a public space should be, what should happen there, and who should have a say in its ongoing management. But even this cursory glance at the redesign of Federal Plaza shows that looking at successive changes to public spaces reveals more than would the examination of individual designs in isolation. These two projects, *Tilted Arc* and Jacob Javits Plaza, have not been examined together as part of the site's ongoing and contentious history. Discussions regarding *Tilted Arc* have not been part of landscape-architecture criticism. Rather, they have been conducted within the realms of art criticism or social criticism. Schwartz's plaza was mainly discussed in landscape-architecture writing, with only superficial references to the *Tilted Arc* saga.

One could argue that this separation is warranted, since the two projects shared little other than a physical location. Serra's *Tilted Arc* was a massive COR-TEN steel minimalist sculpture inserted within a preexisting plaza (Figure 2.1). Schwartz's project, which remains in place today, involved a complete plaza redesign, from building edge to sidewalk: new purple paving, swirls of back-to-back bright green benches, blue enamel water fountains, curlicue handrails, streetlights double their normal height, and giant mounds of grass that give off puffs of water vapor (Figure 2.2). Whereas *Tilted Arc* was minimal, sober, and massive, Schwartz's plaza is elaborate, jaunty, and colorful.

The ongoing history of Federal Plaza, including Serra's and Schwartz's designs and the debates that led to the demolition of Serra's *Tilted Arc* and to the construction of Schwartz's redesign, expose more about the politics of public space than does either event on its own. What is surprising in the Federal Plaza case is not simply that discourse and design are part of the same processes of cultural production—processes that determine the relationship between a public space and its public spheres—rather, it is astonishing that they are in many instances not clearly recognized as such by those people

Figure 2.1. Federal Plaza and *Tilted Arc*, February 1987. Courtesy of Marc Treib.

ART OR LUNCH?

Figure 2.2. Jacob Javits Plaza, November 2000.

engaged in the very physical transformation of public space. The Federal Plaza case is an example of the inability or unwillingness of design criticism and practice to engage with public spaces as the sites and subjects of active public spheres.

## Tilted Arcs and Curving Benches

While the fate of *Tilted Arc* may be familiar to many, two important aspects of the story are less obvious. First, this story offers a graphic example of how physical changes are made to spaces based on arguments about who the public is and what is in their interest. Second, the sculpture and its subsequent removal spurred political and academic discussions about issues, including the importance of public spaces tied to public buildings, the role of public art, and what constitutes public process. Together, these factors create a second story about *Tilted Arc* and its site, a story about diverse constituencies intervening in the creation of a public space. In other words, because of its removal, *Tilted Arc* generated a kind of public sphere.

Completed in 1967, 26 Federal Plaza was designed by architects Alfred Easton Poor, Kahn and Jacobs, and Eggers and Higgins. The building sits within New York's civic center, the hub of government office buildings in the city. Two blocks away from City Hall, the Federal Building is bordered by Broadway to the west, and Foley Square to the east. Other civic buildings facing Foley Square include Surrogate's Court, the Municipal Building, the U.S. Courthouse, and the New York County Court. The Federal Building houses about 10,000 employees in nearly 2.8 million gross square feet and is the second-largest civilian federal office building in the country.[2] When it opened, the Federal Building was called "a microcosm of the Government"[3] because of the concentration of federal offices it held, including the Department of Agriculture, the Securities and Exchange Commission, the Interstate Commerce Commission, and the National Labor Relations Board.

With forty-one floors, the building remains one of the tallest in the civic center. The building is easily spotted because of its stature and the pattern created on its surface by its zigzagging rows of windows. A large plaza sits on the building's eastern side. When the plaza was originally designed, it had a large working fountain and its paving was patterned after Roman designs—in particular, Michelangelo's work at the Campidoglio in Rome.[4] While creating a European-style plaza may have been the architects' intention, commentators on Federal Plaza found the plaza lacking.[5] In a 1985 *New York Times* article, Paul Goldberger described the plaza as "an ugly space bordered by undistinguished buildings and centered, more or less, by an empty pool and dry fountain," adding, "in a city of bad plazas in front of bad skyscrapers, this is one of the worst. Federal Plaza is a dreary stretch of concrete, punctuated by a poorly placed and poorly designed fountain; it was no urban oasis by a long shot."[6] Because it was built over the top of a parking garage whose structure could not bear the additional weight, the plaza had no trees. The fountain proved difficult to maintain, and was eventually turned off altogether. It may not have been a place where people wanted to linger, particularly after the fountain broke, because of the wind in the winter or the heat in the summer. The space was large and open enough, however, for protests and demonstrations. In 1971, for example, federal employees rallied there to protest a Nixon wage freeze.[7] In this way, the plaza's openness was an asset. It allowed the space to be used as the site for certain public spheres.

In 1979, through the GSA's Art-in-Architecture program, the U.S. General Services Administration (GSA) commissioned Richard Serra to design a sculpture for 26 Federal Plaza.[8] Under this program, one-half of 1 percent of the cost of any new building or building under construction is required to be set aside for the incorporation of fine art. Though the Federal

Building was constructed in 1967, more than ten years before Serra's *Tilted Arc* was installed in 1981, no art was commissioned at the time of its initial construction because the Art-in-Architecture program had been at the time temporarily suspended. A controversy over Robert Motherwell's 1966 Boston mural, stemming from a false report that the mural was an abstract image of the assassination of President Kennedy,[9] led the GSA to stop the program for six years.[10] When the Federal Building was to be remodelled more than ten years later, a National Education Association (NEA) panel included Serra in a list of potential artists for the site, and the GSA approved him and his concept for his piece. Ironically, Serra's sculpture ultimately drew more ire than Motherwell's mural did.

Because of its style, scale, material, and position, it's not surprising that *Tilted Arc* drew such criticism and became one of the most controversial works of public art in the United States. The piece consisted of a long slab of steel that stretched across the plaza in a shallow curve. Unlike many sculptures in public spaces in New York City, *Tilted Arc* was not representational; it did not depict a historic moment or figure. *Tilted Arc* was, therefore, difficult to view and to interpret as art. Though these features were in keeping with the sculpture's minimalist style, even within the genre of minimalism *Tilted Arc* stood out. The very material it was made out of also caused unease. COR-TEN steel is fabricated to rust, a finish most equate with scrap metal or waste, not with fine art. *Tilted Arc* also appeared uncontained. It did not sit on a pedestal, but rather appeared to come out of the plaza itself. It did not even stand upright, but rather angled in toward its concave side, giving passersby the feeling that it might somehow fall and crush them while at the same time appearing firmly rooted to the plaza's surface. Because of its shape and position, the sculpture looked very different depending from which side of the plaza you viewed it. From one angle, its entire length appeared; from another, the thinness of the slab and the shape of the curve became more visible.

To those unfamiliar with the history of *Tilted Arc* it might seem logical that when William Diamond, the New York regional administrator of the GSA, said, "this is a day for the people to rejoice, because now the plaza returns rightly to the people," he was referring to the day the sculpture was unveiled. This was not the case, however; he made the statement upon the sculpture's removal. Two days before the statement was published in the *New York Post*, a crew worked through the night sawing and torching the 120-foot-long, twelve-foot-high, several-inch-thick COR-TEN steel curve.[11] The

ART OR LUNCH?

pieces are still held in government storage.[12] Diamond's statement, though perhaps overdramatic, indicates that the *Tilted Arc* controversy was directly tied to the idea that the physical qualities of a place, including art and design, could "remove" a space from "the people." Put differently, art and design can make and unmake public space.

Photographs of the sculpture's demolition and of the arc-shaped cut left in the plaza after its removal illustrate the outcome of an eight-year legal battle between the artist and the client. Hundreds of newspaper and journal articles published up to, during, and well after the sculpture's removal indicate that the piece and its fate remain symbols for those who fought either for its longevity or its demolition.[13] While some of this writing examined the "rights" of an artist in the face of the dismantling of his work, much of it dealt with an underlying ideal of public space.

*Tilted Arc* quickly became one of the most controversial works of public art in the United States. Serra's most vocal and powerful detractors, whose combined efforts led to the sculpture's dismantling, were Judge Edward D. Re, chief judge of the U.S. Court of International Trade, and Ronald Reagan–appointee William Diamond, the GSA's New York regional administrator. In August 1981, the same year that *Tilted Arc* was installed, Judge Re sent a letter to GSA Administrator Gerald Carmen, calling the sculpture "the rusted steel barrier in front of our courthouse." Re argued that it "destroys not only the beauty and spaciousness, but also the utility of the plaza, which has been used for ceremonies."[14]

In 1985, Diamond convened a hearing to decide whether or not *Tilted Arc* should be relocated in order to increase what he called the "public use" of the plaza. Diamond appointed himself as chairperson for the hearing, and appointed the panel members who would debate the question. Diamond sent out hearing announcements that stated, "the purpose of the hearing is to decided whether or not the art work known as *Tilted Arc* . . . should be relocated to increase public use of the plaza."[15] The official GSA public-hearing notice contained similar language: "The General Services Administration is contemplating relocating the artwork . . . to increase public use of the plaza."[16] A flier distributed in the Federal Building prior to the hearing read, "The GSA will hold a public meeting on ways to more fully utilize the plaza. . . . This could include the relocation of the large metal sculpture known as *Tilted Arc*."[17] A petition titled "For Relocation," which circulated before the hearing, stated: "We, the undersigned feel that the artwork called *Tilted Arc* is an obstruction to the plaza and should be removed to a more suitable location."[18]

**29**

The petition also indicated that those who thought that *Tilted Arc* had no artistic merit should put an asterisk next to their name.

Hearing testimonies against Serra's work most often cited dislike for the aesthetics of the sculpture. They described *Tilted Arc* as "a wall of steel," "a rusted metal wall," or "a scar on the plaza"; they stated that it should be "relocated to a better site—a metal salvage yard" or that its removal would "reprieve us from our desolate condemnation."[19] One person commented that it sent the wrong message to people visiting the building to apply for U.S. citizenship, because it reminded people of the "iron curtains from which they escape . . . they should not be compelled to circumvent a rusty reminder of totalitarianism."[20]

Many commentators paired the sculpture's ugliness with the idea that because it was so imposing, it prevented the plaza from being used as a place for relaxing or special events, which in turn created a kind of double argument: people were repelled from the plaza because of the sculpture, and therefore the plaza could no longer function as a public space. One official with offices in the Federal Building stated:

> I . . . remember my dreams of additional seating areas, of more cultural events, temporary outdoor exhibits of sculptures and paintings, ethnic dance festivals and children's shows. All of those things are just memories now, ending with the installation of *Tilted Arc*. . . . The *Arc* has condemned us to lead emptier lives.[21]

Others, who did not comment on the merits of *Tilted Arc* as a work of art, argued that its size prevented people from using the plaza. A representative of Community Board 1, in which Federal Plaza sits, stated that the board voted in favor of removing *Tilted Arc* because it "obstructs most of the open space . . . and both dissuades and denies the public most uses that the public plaza could be used for. . . . Mr. Serra's sculpture has . . . contributed to the public's rejection of this space."[22]

Serra and his supporters argued that removal of the sculpture was tantamount to its destruction, given that *Tilted Arc* was a site-specific work. It was argued that "The specificity of site-oriented works means that they are conceived for, dependent upon, and inseparable from their location."[23] In support of this claim, Serra noted that at Federal Plaza the sun moved across the site in the same direction that the workers moved into the adjacent Federal Building. He argued that he planned the sculpture "so that there would be no shadows from the sculpture at midday . . . thus maximiz[ing] the

ART OR LUNCH?

sculptural condition when some people gather in the plaza."[24] Serra set up the arc's endpoints to mirror the curve of the plaza steps, with "curve answering curve," creating "an amphitheater-like space, where the steps could easily function as seats."[25] In elevation, the metal arc tilts to the eye level of workers or visitors as they exit the building, thereby "establishing a consciousness and condition of human scale."[26] Standing in the doorway, the height of the arc was set to appear similar to the height of the columns of the building and the portals of the doorways, "thus connecting the framing of the building to the elevation of the sculpture."[27]

While Serra and his supporters emphasised the site-specific nature of *Tilted Arc* in arguing against its relocation, they downplayed claims of the sculpture's aggressive character.[28] In an interview with art historian Douglas Crimp, Serra suggested that he had intentionally designed *Tilted Arc* to be massive and imposing, stating:

> It is necessary to work in opposition to the constraints of the context, so that the work cannot be read as an affirmation of questionable ideologies and political power. I am not interested in art as an affirmation or complicity.[29]

Serra and his supporters unsuccessfully countered the "public use" argument by asserting that events on the site were infrequent. They argued that the physical location of the sculpture did not preclude such events from happening in the future and that the state of the site prior to the installation of *Tilted Arc* was so inhuman in scale that it was inappropriate for events anyway. Douglas Crimp observed:

> The designers of the Federal Plaza managed to create a space that was inhuman in its scale, and in the way the wind whips through. The fountain could never be turned on because it would completely sweep the plaza with water. . . . They were talking about how *Tilted Arc* prevented all these wonderful events from happening on the plaza, but we knew what bad faith that was. Have they organized public concerts in the plaza since?[30]

In his hearing testimony and in later interviews, Crimp argued that the GSA pushed the "use" versus "sculpture" argument to develop a false sense of divisiveness between government workers and the artists who lived and worked in the neighborhood. He wrote, "I believe that we have been polarized here in order that we not notice the real issue: the fact that our social experience is deliberately and drastically limited by our public officials."[31] Crimp went on to argue that part of the merit of *Tilted Arc* is that it brought these issues to light:

> I urge that we keep this wall in place and that we construct our social experience in relation to it, that is, out of the sights of those who would conceive of social life as something to be feared, despised, and surveyed.[32]

Crimp elaborates Serra's position that art can change social habits. Left in place, Serra's sculpture might challenge us to walk, act, think differently. But to Crimp the "publicness" of public space is tied neither to aesthetics nor government designation. Neither artists nor officials make public space.

> The plaza is defined as it is used by a public. If a public takes over that space and holds political meetings or rock concerts, then it becomes public through that use.[33]

By arguing that public space is generated through public actions, Crimp emphasizes its dynamic nature. He underscores the fact that no matter how a plaza is designed, if government officials limit how it can be used, it is not a public space.

Art historian Rosalyn Deutsche also discusses the GSA's manufacture of a conflict between the public use of the space and the obstacle of Serra's sculpture.[34] But Deutsche emphasizes that the very terms *public* and *use* can be used to control public space. For Deutsche, the significant issue of these debates was not the questions of whether the government had the authority to remove *Tilted Arc,* whether Serra's piece was "good public art," or whether the space allowed for public events. Rather, the debates show how the GSA controlled public discourse and, therefore, public space through rhetorical means. The GSA chose *not* to define *public* and *use* in explicit or precise terms. Instead, they presented them as givens, as implicitly understood terms. For Deutsche, public space is the site of democracy. It is not just that we live in a democratic society and therefore that we should maintain openness in public space, but rather that public space *is* the democratic realm. It is the "place" where democracy happens.[35]

> Categories like "the public" can, of course, be construed as naturally or fundamentally coherent only by disavowing the conflicts, particularity, heterogeneity, and uncertainty that constitute social life. But when participants in a debate about the

uses of public space remove the definitions of public and use to a realm of objectivity located not only outside the *Tilted Arc* debate but also outside debate altogether, they threaten to erase public space itself. For what initiates debate about social questions if not the absence of absolute sources of meaning and the concomitant recognition that these questions—including the question of the meaning of public space—are decided only in a public space?[36]

Hearing testimony in favor of Serra's work focused on issues related to the aesthetic merit of the work itself and resisted questions about how the GSA's decisions indicated a desire for control of the plaza:

> While the *Tilted Arc* debate frequently included complex material critiques of art's production and of aesthetic perception, it nonetheless obstructed interrogation of the conditions of production of New York's urban space.[37]

As Deutsche and Crimp argue, unquestioned definitions of terms *public* and *use* can be used to control discourse about public space. This point is of great importance to design practitioners and critics and could have informed the next phase of design and criticism of Federal Plaza. Public space is both physical and rhetorical. Rhetoric can be used to control who is and who is not considered part of the public. Rhetoric can claim incontestable uses of spaces that exclude groups and individuals. If you are not there for the concert, why are you in the space? If you are not part of the ceremony, why are you in the plaza? While a landscape architect might design a space that has the flexibility to support varied uses, that offers physical accessibility, that provides spaces that can be temporarily co-opted by different individuals and groups, that same site can be made equally *inaccessible* by what constitutes appropriate "use."

Criticism was central to the history of *Tilted Arc*. Criticism defined, challenged, and redefined public space. Criticism influenced physical changes at Federal Plaza and positioned the history of *Tilted Arc* within larger debates about the politics of public space. For Serra, it was more important that *Tilted Arc* be confrontational than pleasing, since the purpose of the sculpture was to criticize political power. To Re and Diamond, the purpose of public art and public space was to provide comfortable settings for relaxation, not to challenge the power of government institutions. Hearing participants developed critical strategies to argue against Re's and Diamond's assertions. Crimp and Deutsche developed standpoints on the role of public art and public space based on a critical appraisal of the sculpture and the rhetoric that prefigured its destruction. The next iteration of Federal Plaza and its history constitute an additional set of critical responses and physical changes to the site. These responses did not, however, take into account the central questions framed by *Tilted Arc*. Rather, they seem to have accepted the GSA's static framing of public space as a place where people engage in prescribed sets of activities. As a result, when Federal Plaza was transformed into Jacob Javits Plaza, it was not conceived of as the potential site or subject of public spheres.

## Jacob Javits Plaza and the Use of Public Space

In 1992 the GSA hired Martha Schwartz to redesign the plaza. At this time, the site was renamed Jacob Javits Plaza in honor of a former U.S. senator. Schwartz completely transformed the space. What was once an open, if inhospitable, area is now filled with oversized furnishings bordered at the building edge by a broad path and antiterrorist bollards. In the main portion of the plaza, six swirls of bright green benches and six giant grass-covered mounds create a kind of broad maze. The mounds were designed to give off mist on hot days. The mounds and benches take up much of the surface of the plaza, which is also dotted with blue enamel water fountains, orange mesh garbage cans, and tall black lights. The surface is covered with swirls of purple-and-black paving. Around the edges of the plaza nearest the sidewalk Schwartz installed a series of steps where the sidewalk was lower. The steps' handrails end in huge black metal curves. Changes have been made to Schwartz's project. The grass mounds are now covered with boxwood and no longer emit puffs of water vapor.

Critical responses to Schwartz's redesign reiterated the idea that *Tilted Arc* prevented the public from using the plaza. Art critics who were so vocal during the *Tilted Arc* hearings have not responded to Schwartz's redesign. Landscape-architecture critics and historians have written about Schwartz's work, but not in the critical context set out by Deutsche and Crimp. Instead, their arguments represent GSA-sponsored attitudes about the role of design in public space and in public life. Articles on Jacob Javits Plaza found in *Landscape Architecture*, the *New York Times*, the *New Yorker*, and *Land Forum*, and the Spacemaker Press monograph *Martha Schwarz: Transfiguration of the Commonplace*[38] contain rhetoric similar to that used by the GSA in their testimony against *Tilted Arc*. Such writings commonly state that the presence of *Tilted Arc* precluded any other use of the space. Similarly, art and landscape architecture critic John Beardsley describes Schwartz's work as follows: "There is no question about the fact that Schwartz has designed a more user-friendly space than Serra's; she has replaced metaphors of conflict with those of leisure."[39] And while Beardsley states that he regretted that Schwartz's design completely erased from the site any indication of *Tilted Arc,* he adds, "I suppose it's reasonable to put a limit on the debate—as Schwartz says, 'We've picked that scab long enough. It's time to move on.'"[40]

It is ironic that Schwartz refers to debate as a scab that won't heal. Perhaps more important than leaving a physical marker indicating the former presence of *Tilted Arc* would have been for Schwartz's project and critical responses to it to revive the discussions raised during the legal battle over Serra's sculpture and to take on the difficult question of what a public space in front of a major public building might be. Instead, Schwartz's plaza and the rhetoric surrounding it gave permanent form to a GSA-approved definition of public and appropriate use. This definition emerged out of a distorted interpretation of the site's contentious history. Articles on Schwartz's company's Web site,[41] in *Landscape Architecture,*[42] the Spacemaker Press monograph on Martha Schwartz, and the *Land Forum* "Rants and Raves" article[43] include false, misleading, or uncritical readings of the site's contentious history. For example, the article announcing Schwartz's 1997 American Society of Landscape Architects Award for Jacob Javits Plaza reads: "[w]hatever the inherent merits of *Tilted Arc,* its location on the plaza was both a visual and physical obstruction for pedestrians and its presence effectively precluded any other use of the space."[44] The brief description of Jacob Javits Plaza by Martha Schwartz, included with photographs and a plan published in the Spacemaker Press monograph on Martha Schwarz, reiterates the idea that the sculpture was removed because it conflicted with the site's use. The questions raised by Deutsche's and Crimp's writings regarding how the words *public* and *use* are defined or deployed are buried again.

With so much attention being paid to how Federal Plaza could have been a place that people could "use," it is ironic and perhaps shocking that the final design prescribed such a narrow program. In actuality, only one use is described by Schwartz: eating lunch.

> "At first I was outraged . . . but I came to feel sorry for those who had to use the space" . . . she developed what she called "an antithetical sort of piece." "I would shape the space for the way people actually use it: to eat lunch."[45]

Weekday lunchtime is the only programmed use that is mentioned; its design elements include "[f]amiliar lunchtime paraphernalia—blue enamelled drinking fountains, Central Park light stands, and orange wire-mesh trash cans—occupy the surface."[46]

The "lunchtime paraphernalia" and benches take up so much of the available space that sitting and eating may be the only use possible. As the plan view indicates, Schwartz's plaza is filled with loops of benches. The curves of the benches are meant to "allow for a variety of seating—intimate circles for groups and flat outside curves for those who wish to lunch alone."[47] But their size and positioning make crossing the plaza very difficult. There is only one direct route across the plaza, and that route is only visible as such from one point along the sidewalk. The benches also make large-scale events such as concerts and demonstrations almost impossible. One might argue that concertgoers could sit on the benches, but their configuration is so multidirectional that the majority of people seated would be facing the wrong direction.

Landscape-architecture critics, including Clare Cooper-Marcus, have even questioned how successful Schwartz was in satisfying the needs of such a limited constituency. In her letter to *Landscape Architecture* titled "Statement vs. Design," Cooper-Marcus charged that Schwartz's plaza fell short of its goal of providing space to eat lunch, citing too much seating, an inappropriate scale of the seating arcs for intimate gathering, and the empty look of the site.

> Endless swirling back-to-back benches set in mauve concrete with
> orange trash containers—is that the kind of space in which you
> would want to eat lunch? Is this the kind of setting where someone
> working under fluorescent light bulbs in front of a computer
> screen in an air-conditioned office would want to go to relax . . .
> a perusal of William Whyte's *Social Life of Small Urban Places* . . .
> would suggest to the designer and her clients that "eating lunch"
> has many, many more subtle design implications than merely
> providing endless benches and eye-catching trash containers.[48]

In defense of her design, Schwartz drew attention to the fact that the "public" was consulted in the design process. They asked for and got lots of seating. Other critics commented that the mist from the green hills counted as a water feature, as advocated by William Whyte, and that artistic design improves public space.[49]

ART OR LUNCH?

Whether or not it is a pleasant place to eat lunch, the "public" of Jacob Javits Plaza includes more than lunching office workers. In addition to housing the GSA, the Federal Building also houses offices, including offices for the Social Security Administration, Immigration and Naturalization Services (INS), and the U.S. Army Corps of Engineers. Because of the presence of these offices, there is considerable pedestrian movement through the plaza. While the *Tilted Arc* hearings referred to two sets of "publics"—namely, the office workers and the artists who lived in loft spaces in Tribeca—there is at least one more "set," according to Douglas Crimp:

> there is another group on the site every day that outnumber either of these groups: people from all over New York who need a green card, a new driver's license, who must meet a court date, or serve on jury duty.[50]

Crimp's point is emphasized in a series of newspaper articles that enlarge the scope of the plaza's potential public, including groups as diverse as people forced to spend the night on the sidewalk next to the plaza in order to line up for an appointment at INS, and the 10,000 to 20,000 demonstrators who marched from Brooklyn to Federal Plaza to protest police brutality.[51]

The plaza is managed strictly. People are not allowed to demonstrate there. But the dominance of the physical objects within the plaza also severely limits what can happen. There is simply no space for even GSA-approved uses of ceremonies and concerts. Serra's sculpture occupied less of the plaza than Schwartz's redesign (Figures 2.3 and 2.4). There is now not enough room for events such as large-scale government demonstrations and protests. Even if a group could secure permission to hold an event there, the physical layout and the design elements of Jacob Javits Plaza would limit how many people could participate and what they could do there.

Ironically, the reason given for the repetition and oversized forms of the benches and other furnishings that crowd the space of the plaza today is that they are Schwartz's critical commentary on public space. Schwartz's work is broadly considered to be at the cutting edge of the field of landscape architecture because her design work can also be interpreted as *critical* work. What does the design of Jacob Javits Plaza critique? According to promotional material prepared by Martha Schwartz, Inc., the ASLA Award write-up, and an article by Elizabeth Meyers, the design for Jacob Javits Plaza addresses the difficulty of designing a public space in New York,

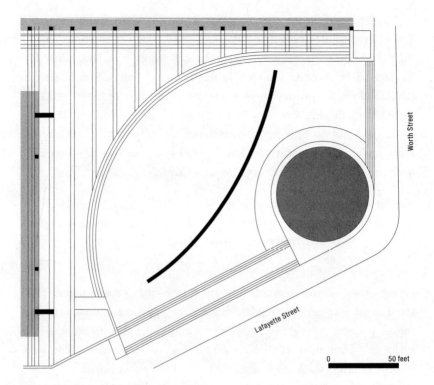

Worth Street

Lafayette Street

0          50 feet

Figure 2.3. Plan view of *Tilted Arc* in Federal Plaza. Drafted by Vincent deBritto.

where contemporary urban landscape design can be reduced to selecting stock items from the Parks Department's list of appropriate materials . . . Schwartz is adopting another strategy for objectifying the public realm. . . . Playing by the rules, Schwartz's design proposal for the Jacob Javits plaza includes, in her words, "traditional New York Park elements with a humorous twist." . . . These elements (the trash cans, light standards, benches and other "lunchtime paraphernalia") offer a critique of the art of landscape in New York City, where the ghost of Frederick Law Olmsted is too great a force for even New York to exercise . . . Javits Plaza is therefore a recognizable park, historic and acceptable to New Yorkers, but its familiar elements have all gone a little mad.[52]

The relevance of this critique to this particular site must be questioned. How important is criticism of street furnishings compared to the discussions of public space and the relationship of public space to democracy, as raised by debate over the appropriateness of the *Tilted Arc*? Schwartz offers Jacob

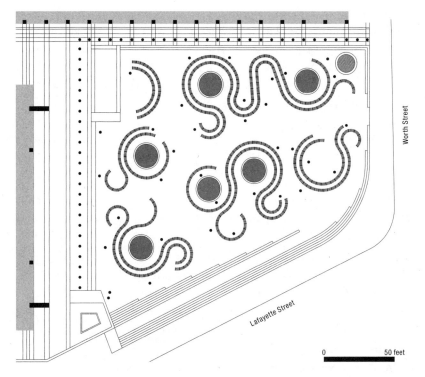

Worth Street

Lafayette Street

0    50 feet

Figure 2.4. Plan view of Jacob Javits Plaza. Drafted by Vincent deBritto.

Javits Plaza as a kind of wry joke on the difficulty of designing in a city that places so much emphasis on a historic *style* of design, suggesting: "I was tweaking New York City's nose. . . . After *Tilted Arc*, I just wanted to give people a nice plaza to eat lunch."[53] The ubiquity of Olmsted's nineteenth-century design style seems of little importance, given the plaza's complex and controversial *recent* history. Schwartz has not only chosen an insubstantial target for critique, but, furthermore, her design gives permanent physical form to the GSA's limited conception of *public*. The GSA's position, revealed in the rhetoric of the *Tilted Arc* hearings and challenged by critics like Deutsche and Crimp, became material space in Jacob Javits Plaza.

On a site that is managed less as a public space and more as a controlled antechamber to the Federal Building, the site's "humorous" appearance is troubling. No written review of the design of Jacob Javits Plaza has argued whether it is now a public space at all. As we saw at City Hall, government ownership does not indicate public accessibility. That is to say, simply because it is a publicly owned space does not mean that it is a public space. The plaza has a history of public access that legally indicates it is a public forum under the First Amendment.[54] However, the GSA does not currently manage it as such. Security issues were raised in the destruction of *Tilted Arc* and guide current management practices (Figure 2.5). It is important to note that the *Tilted Arc* controversies, in which issues of security were raised, and Schwartz's redesign of the plaza both predate the Oklahoma City Federal Building bombing in April 1995 and the bombing of the World Trade Center and the Pentagon in September 2001. In the course of writing this chapter, also prior to 9/11, attempts to take photographs of the plaza revealed the implications of calling Federal Plaza a public space at all. Security workers routinely ask those taking photos to stop or else have their camera confiscated. In order to be allowed to photograph the plaza, one must first enter the Federal Building through a security checkpoint and then report to the building manager's office. There one fills out a form (requiring this permit is, according to the NYCLU, illegal) requesting to hold a special event or art exhibition on the site (Figure 2.6). Thus, even a space so restricted through its design can be further restricted by regulation and policing.

While security may seem an incontestable concern, Crimp points out that the GSA has used this issue in defending its control of the plaza. The GSA, Crimp argues, today uses the issue of security in the same way it used the issue of aesthetics in the events leading to the destruction of *Tilted Arc*—namely, to divide and distract dissenting voices. In the case of security, the GSA is constructing an "other" that is dangerous to the "real" public. As Crimp observed:

> I would submit it is we—the public—who are on the other side
> of the wall, and it is we whom Judge Re so fears and despises that
> he wants that wall torn down in order that we may be properly
> subjected to surveillance.[55]

While it is incorrect to say that certain physical forms lead to a public space, design can limit a person's ability to decide what she would do in a space and how she would do it. Many factors can lead to decisions that limit public space. In the case of Federal Plaza, those factors may have included a desire for greater control, personal dislike of a controversial artwork, and a desire for greater visibility of activities on the plaza. In other cases, decisions may be based on greed, prejudice, or revenge.[56] Crimp fears that: "[T]he William Diamonds of this world . . . want a shrinking public sphere.

Figure 2.5. Security booth and benches, Jacob Javits Plaza, November 2000.

ART OR LUNCH?

**PART I – APPLICATION**

| 1A. FIRST, MIDDLE, LAST NAME OF APPLICANT | 1B. COMPLETE MAILING ADDRESS |
|---|---|
| Kristine F MILLER | 616 LINCOLN AVE ST. PAUL, MIN. 55102 |

| 1C. TELEPHONE NUMBER |
|---|
| 651 292 8137 |

| 2A. NAME OF PERSON OR ORGANIZATION SPONSORING, PROMOTING, OR CONDUCTING THE PROPOSED ACTIVITY | 2B. COMPLETE MAILING ADDRESS |
|---|---|
| University of Minnesota | University Ave, SE Landscape Architecture Minneapolis, MN 55414 |

| 2C. TELEPHONE NUMBER |
|---|
| 612 626 6000 |

| 3A. NAME(S) OF PERSON(S) WHO WILL HAVE SUPERVISION OVER AND RESPONSIBILITY FOR THE PROPOSED ACTIVITY | 3B. COMPLETE MAILING ADDRESS |
|---|---|
| | |

| 3C. TELEPHONE NUMBER |
|---|
| |

4. DESCRIPTION OF PROPOSED ACTIVITY
TAKING PICTURES OF PLAZA. DESIGNED BY MARTHA SCHWARTZ

5. PROPOSED BUILDING AND AREA
JACOB JAVITS PLAZA

| 6. PROPOSED DATES AND HOURS DURING WHICH THE ACTIVITY IS TO BE CARRIED OUT | | | 7. APPROXIMATE NUMBER OF PERSONS TO BE ENGAGED IN THIS ACTIVITY (if known) |
|---|---|---|---|
| A. FROM: 1:00 11/15 | B. TO: 4:30 11/15 | C. HOURS: 3.5 | 1 |

IMPORTANT: If applicant purports to represent an organization, a letter or other documentation that the applicant has authority to represent that organization is required to be submitted with this form.

8. APPLICANTS PROPOSING TO ENGAGE IN THE SOLICITATION OF FUNDS MUST CHECK ONE OF THE FOLLOWING STATEMENTS:

I HEREBY CERTIFY THAT:

____ A. I represent and will be soliciting funds for the sole benefit of a religion or religious group;

____ B. My organization has received an official Internal Revenue Service (IRS) ruling or letter of determination stating that the organization or its parent organization qualifies for tax-exempt status under 26 U.S.C. 501 (c)(3), (c)(4), or (c)(5); or

____ C. My organization has applied to the IRS for a determination of tax-exempt status under 26 U.S.C. 501 (c)(3), (c)(4), or (c)(5), and that the IRS has not yet issued a final administrative ruling or determination of such status.

CERTIFICATION: I CERTIFY that the above information is true and correct.

| 9. SIGNATURE OF APPLICANT | 10. DATE SIGNED |
|---|---|
| Kristine M | Nov. 15, 2000 |

**PART II – PERMIT (TO BE COMPLETED ONLY BY GSA)**

11. DESIGNATED BUILDING AND AREA AND ACTUAL DATES AND HOURS FOR WHICH ACTIVITY IS APPROVED

| A. BUILDING AND AREA | B. FROM: | C. TO: | D. HOURS: |
|---|---|---|---|
| Federal Plaza | 11-15-2000 | 11-15-2000 | 4:00hr |

| 12. SIGNATURE OF GSA APPROVING OFFICIAL | 13. DATE SIGNED |
|---|---|
| B.M. | 11/15/2000 |

GENERAL SERVICES ADMINISTRATION          (See Reverse)          GSA FORM 3453 (12-80

Figure 2.6. Permit to hold special event at Jacob Javits Plaza, November 2000.

That's where their power resides."[57] The power of dynamic public space increases and decreases according to how we imagine and create it. When we create constrained places, we limit the possibility for action. When we conceive of a prescribed set of activities, we shut out the potential for a more varied and diverse public life.

ART OR LUNCH?

The ongoing history of design at Federal Plaza clearly illustrates that public space and the public are both physically produced and rhetorically constructed. Rhetoric argues for or against the "appropriateness" of different modes of behavior and activities. Built form reinforces who the public is by limiting how a site can be used. Critics can turn a blind eye to these issues by focusing on a design's physical appearance or by reiterating a firm's promotional stance. This is not to say that *all* parties involved in the production and construction of Jacob Javits Plaza had as their goal the exclusion of groups or individuals from the site. But designers and critics must not unwittingly support the erosion of public space by failing to recognize that broader political issues are at stake. These issues were exposed in the legal battles over *Tilted Arc* and were questioned by Crimp and Deutsche. By not carrying these discussions forward, Jacob Javits Plaza's "whimsical" benches represent a failure of public space design and criticism.

At City Hall, government officials used regulation to control how the steps were used and by whom. At Federal Plaza, the same results were achieved through rhetoric and design. It takes much longer to physically change a space than to enact regulations governing what can happen there, but physical changes are more durable. Regulations can be applied and retracted in days or weeks. Designs exist over longer periods of time. While it is more obvious to a passerby that a space has been redesigned than that a space has been newly regulated, designs are less easily "read" as controls. Redesigning a space is also more costly than setting out new regulations. But because of these costs, new designs are often subject to some kind of review. Review processes and redesigns themselves generate a body of assertions about the role of public space.

Given the fact that physical designs are more intractable and, perhaps, more difficult to analyze, tackling the role of design and critique in public space seems all the more important. But the question remains, what should Schwartz have done? How should she have designed the plaza? The answer, of course, depends on what kind of site and subject of active public realms the plaza should support. Given there is a practically limitless number of people who are affected by U.S. federal policy and who therefore are potentially part of the "public" of Federal Plaza, and if we agree that speech, protest, and demonstration are important forms of expression and should occur at the location of the accountable government body, then at a minimum Federal Plaza should include a large open area. Providing such a platform need not prevent office workers from having lunch. There is plenty of seating on the steps on the north side of the plaza. There is also a tree-covered park, Foley Square, right across the street. This is not to say that a different design could prevent the GSA or any of the building occupants from regulating the space to control speech acts or to prevent people from occupying the space, but we should not ignore the aesthetic power of large-scale open spaces in front of public buildings. The design of Jacob Javits Plaza could have, even in the absence of actual demonstration or protest, reminded us that public spaces are the sites and subjects of public spheres.

At Federal Plaza, we saw how discourse about what should happen in a public space was concretized in built form in a government-controlled location. But what about public spaces that are not directly tied to public buildings? What about design projects that transform entire portions of the city, including not only streets and sidewalks but also buildings and land that are privately owned? In the next chapter, we will move uptown to Times Square to examine the ways in which design, rhetoric, and law transform private and public space alike, according to what is deemed to be in the public's interest.

# 3 Condemning the Public in the New Times Square

> Almost everybody rightly celebrates Times Square's
> revival as one of New York City's greatest recent
> success stories . . . it was sleazy, blighted, and crime-
> ridden; today it . . . bustles with tourists by day and
> night, and world-spanning corporations such as AMC,
> Disney, and Viacom prosper within it.
>   —*William Stern, former New York City police
>   commissioner,* City Journal, *1999*

> The scheme had all the elements of a Joe Orton black
> comedy: a multi-billion-dollar real estate deal that piously
> packaged public morality and profitable mathematics
> under the banner of Times Square cleanup, and an
> unbelievable rerun of discredited 1960's urban renewal.
>   —*Ada Louise Huxtable, "Times Square Renewal (Act II),
>   a Farce,"* New York Times, *October 14, 1989*

**The name "Times Square"** refers both to a location within the city and to an icon. Stretching north to Fifty-third Street, south to Fortieth Street, east to Sixth Avenue, and west to Eighth Avenue, Times Square includes roughly twenty-five blocks of the borough of Manhattan.[1] Two of the most famous streets in the United States cross here: Broadway and Forty-second Street. Once known as the Great White Way, Broadway is home to American theater. Forty-second Street, once called the Dangerous Deuce, is infamous for its history as the city's vice capital.[2] Each New Year's Eve, most North American televisions are tuned in to watch the Times Square ball drop, signaling the first party of the year.

The redevelopment of Times Square began in the mid-1970s and continues today. Over a thirty-year period, cheap restaurants, second-run movie houses, small business offices and peep shows, and low-rise buildings were replaced with theme restaurants, toy stores, television studios, and hotel towers. The transformation included a renaming of the district from "Times Square" to "the New Times Square." Millions of tourists pass through every day to see the stories-tall neon and LCD signs and to visit megastores such as Toys-R-Us, which features a giant indoor Ferris wheel.

In part because of its iconic status, the New Times Square has become a kind of poster child both for its boosters and its detractors. Its boosters, such as former New York City Police Commissioner Robert Stern, claim that the New Times Square proves that cities can reform "blighted" neighborhoods by attracting corporate developers through the promise of large developable land parcels acquired through eminent domain. Its detractors claim that the Times Square redevelopment approach bears a striking resemblance to 1960s–1970s urban renewal, in which low-income areas were demolished to make way for highways, convention centers, and high-rise housing projects. Both arguments are correct. However, each views in very different ways who the public of Times Square is and what their best interest is.

Both City Hall and Federal Plaza were well-defined physical locations attached to important government buildings. In each case, government officials used regulation and discourse to control the public of the space. But what about public spaces that are not bound by publicly owned buildings? What is the role of government agencies in determining appropriate uses and therefore appropriate public bodies across much larger geographies— geographies bordered by private, not public, buildings? This chapter addresses not a set of steps or a plaza, but several city blocks. Like the steps of City Hall, Times Square's public was transformed through the use of regulation and law. Like Federal Plaza, Times Square was transformed through design. The Times Square story shows that the combination of law and design transforms public space much more powerfully than either element in isolation.

In Times Square, the letter and practice of law *combined* with the rhetoric and practice of design define, delineate, and reproduce imagined and actual public bodies and public spaces. Unlike at City Hall, the laws in play in Times Square did not relate to the right to speak but to the right of the state to forcibly purchase private property for projects deemed to be "in the public's interest." Unlike Federal Plaza, the redesign of Times Square was not limited to one plaza or even one design field. At Times Square, urban design, architecture, landscape architecture, and graphic design were all employed. The questions raised by the Times Square case are complex. How do laws governing the taking of private property relate to public spaces? Do questions of access and use relate to both small-scale public spaces and across entire portions of a city? How do varied design practices generate public spaces and public bodies? How do we compare the rhetoric of law with the rhetoric of design?

Both law and design were inextricable parts of the same process: defining a public for the New Times Square. By determining what was "in the public interest," eminent-domain case law set out two opposing publics: a criminal public and an idealized general public. By selectively editing and promoting the Times Square public's desires and behaviors, design helped define and represent new moral norms.

## Demolition and the Public's Interest

The Times Square redevelopment process was tumultuous, complex, and controversial. It spanned the tenures of three city mayors and two state governors. In *Reconstructing Times Square: Politics and Culture in Urban Development*,[3] Alex Reichl describes how key players—including then-mayor Ed Koch, the *New York Times*, and real estate corporations—manipulated key demographics to build and sway a tenuous coalition. Historic preservation[4] and design were important carrots that Koch and his team waved in front of the noses of well-educated, white, middle-class constituents; constituents who, Reichl notes, might have otherwise sided with local Times Square community groups and business owners who criticized the project. After all, Koch's plan to condemn and demolish almost three city blocks of largely minority-used shops, apartments, and restaurants and to replace them with offices for white-collar (and white-skinned) workers would have stirred dissent among many well-off, liberal New Yorkers.[5]

While promises of a new and improved cultural district in Times Square helped convince some New Yorkers of the benefits of redevelopment, Times Square property owners reacted to plans for the condemnation and demolition of their properties with over forty lawsuits. These lawsuits and the court decisions that followed indicated that eminent domain—the law itself and its application—legally define the public's interest and physically transform both private and public spaces. Eminent domain law ties the material demolition and rebuilding of a neighborhood to a moral argument about the public good.

## Condemnation in the Public's Interest

Eminent domain in the United States is the power of the state to take private property for public use. Owners whose property is taken must be compensated. Inherent to the idea of eminent domain is that it is right for the state, when acting in the public interest, to forcibly purchase private land, transforming, in theory if not in practice,[6] private space into public space.

One would imagine that in a country in which private property has a privileged status, the conditions under which property can be taken would be clearly delineated and defined. However, this is not the case. The description of eminent domain in the New York Consolidated Laws provides more detail on rules for the just compensation of property owners than on what constitutes appropriate public interest.[7] It is not that terms like *public interest* are broadly defined in the statute. Rather, they are almost undefined. Section 103 of the Consolidated Laws states that a public project "means any program or project for which acquisition of property may be required for a public use, benefit or purpose." The vagueness of the statute gives the legislative branches of state and local government wide latitude in evaluating individual projects. Judges, for the most part, have refused to rule on whether a project is of sufficient public benefit to warrant the taking of private property.

In their project description, the New York State Urban Development Corporation (UDC)[8] listed, in vague language, reasons why the use of eminent domain on Forty-second Street was in the public interest:

> Whereas, The Project Area is marked by street crime, substandard and insanitary [sic] conditions, uses that inhibit the general public's use and enjoyment of the Project Area, and physical, economic and social blight which contribute to the growth of crime and delinquency and impair the sound growth and development of the Project Area and of the City as a whole; and . . . Whereas, The redevelopment of the Project Area is in the best interest of the City in that it will remove blight and physical, economic and social decay and replace them with a variety of new uses which will result in commercial and economic expansion, cultural and entertainment rejuvenation and improved public services and facilities, to the betterment of the Project Area in particular and the City in general.[9]

It is important to note the use of the term *project area*. Terms like *community* or *neighborhood* are not used in eminent domain discourse. In this way, the new, the redeveloped, the expected are favored over existing relationships and social networks. *Project area* also implicates a project that will occur across this area, which itself implicates design.

The UDC also made an implicit distinction between the current public of Times Square and an idealized public that existed elsewhere. The UDC argued that the current public engaged in crime and delinquent behavior, contributed to "social decay," and engaged in "uses that inhibit the general public's use and enjoyment of the Project Area."[10] Oddly, this passage does not refer to actual people. It is as if the bad things were simply happening on their own. Instead of referring to criminals, the UDC refers to crime. Instead of delinquents, it refers to delinquency. In this way the report tied the social and economic conditions in Times Square to the neighborhood itself—its buildings, bad sanitation, etc.—and the uses these settings helped bring about. The distinction between referring to individuals and to generalized problems tied to a material location is significant because it allowed the state to argue that Times Square could be improved by transforming its physical qualities.

One legal reason for condemnation stipulated in the Consolidated Laws on eminent domain and used in Times Square was "blight." The UDC used the term "blight" paired with "decay" to describe the conditions present in Times Square that made redevelopment necessary. Given the UDC's argument that the physical and material conditions present in Times Square had to be changed in order for the social and economic conditions to change, *blight* was a uniquely useful term. *Blight* can refer simultaneously to objects and to processes of a material, social, or medical nature:

> **Blight 1.** gen. Any baleful influence of atmospheric or invisible origin, that suddenly blasts, nips, or destroys plants, affects them with disease, arrests their growth, or prevents their blossom from "setting"; a diseased state of plants of unknown or assumed atmospheric origin. 2. Specifically applied to: a. Diseases in plants caused by fungoid parasites, as mildew, rust, or smut, in corn. 3. Applied to affections of the face or skin: a. An eruption on the human skin consisting of minute reddish pimples, "a form of Lichen urticatus." 4. transf. and fig. a. Any malignant influence of obscure or mysterious origin; anything which withers hopes or prospects, or checks prosperity. b. spec. An unsightly urban area (cf. BLIGHTED ppl. a. 1b).[11]

Blight is "baleful"; blight inspires fear. It can be of "atmospheric . . . invisible . . . obscure . . . mysterious . . . unknown origins." The onset of blight happens "suddenly." It "blasts . . . destroys . . . arrests . . . withers." It "checks prosperity." Blight is also ugly; it "prevents blossoms from setting," consists of "minute reddish pimples," appears "unsightly." Blight connects "withered hopes," "check(ed) prosperity," and "mysterious origins." The presence of blight indicates specific remedies. Blighted and decaying plants are treated by removing the affected portion. Blighted neighborhoods are physically cleared and rebuilt. In effect the UDC was proposing a kind of city surgery, in which the bad part needed to be cut out to save the good (Figure 3.1).[12]

When applied to Times Square, the *blight* label was difficult to contest because the image of Times Square as dirty and dangerous is embedded in American minds. Similarly, the idea that poor people, and especially poor people of color, are bad, dangerous, and immoral and that their conditions/problems may be contagious is not

Figure 3.1. Map of Times Square. Drafted by Vincent deBritto. Courtesy of Forty-second Street Development Project, Inc.

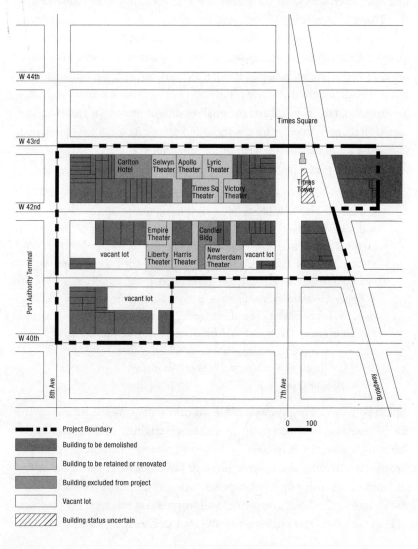

CONDEMNING THE PUBLIC

something particular to a New York brand of racism. Following the logic of the blight argument, the removal of blight and the buildings and people that are part of it would allow a new, healthy, and moral public to take its place. By stating that the project area was not meeting its economic potential, the UDC indicated that this new public also needed to be wealthier. The new commercial interests would need a new/different public body to market to and sell to. This new public needed to be wealthy enough to spend $100.00 on a Broadway show or $40.00 on a new sweatshirt, rather than $5.00 on a second-run movie or $10.00 on a T-shirt. As Samuel Delany, author of *Times Square Red, Times Square Blue,* has argued, pre-redevelopment Times Square was one of New York City's few affordable entertainment districts. By increasing the "profitability" of the neighborhood, the UDC would put Times Square entertainment venues out of reach of many New Yorkers.

The UDC's arguments for increasing the "economic potential" of Times Square were, however, misleading. Current property owners made fairly high rent revenues because the pornography theaters were able to pay them.[13] Furthermore, all of the building owners were paying their property taxes. Current building owners were reluctant to allow the UDC to buy them out *because* they were making money. They also stood to make more money by speculating on their property's future value rather than selling to the government at a time when the prices were low compared to the prices garnered in neighboring districts.

The UDC was also never able to prove that the presence of pornography businesses in Times Square caused its higher levels of crime.[14] In an effort to hold on to their property, some Times Square building owners offered to upgrade facilities and to switch from pornographic to "legitimate" theater.[15] These offers were refused.

In the forty-two lawsuits resulting from the UDC's bid to use eminent domain in Times Square almost all the property owners argued that the redevelopment project was not based on suitable public interest and that the proposed project would suit private interests much more than it would create public gain. Judges repeatedly refused to discuss the public-interest question because, they stated, the legislative body had already proved that the project was in the public interest and it was up to the courts to decide if appropriate processes had been followed and if owners were justly compensated.[16] As Lynne B. Sagalyn notes in *Times Square Roulette,* over fifty-six lawyers were involved in condemnation hearings and litigation regarding just compensation even after some property owners had accepted the state's initial offer. And even after all the properties were legally held by the state, it was another six years before the last tenant was removed.[17] In the midst of the mid-1990s economic recession, demolition began.

Part of the challenge of writing about the development of Times Square is that it took place over an almost thirty-year period. During that time, proposals for what should be done and by whom swung from the construction of four white, monolithic towers designed by architects Philip Johnson and John Burgee,[18] to the New Times Square we see today, with its dazzling array of advertisements that wrap a stylized mix of tourist traps, offices, and entertainment venues. The designers who conceived the idea were graphic designer Tibor Kalman and architect and urban designer Robert M. Stern. The UDC brought in Kalman and Stern when it became clear that a glut in the New York City office-space market had made the Johnson and Burgee plan unfeasible. Kalman and Stern brought a new set of ideas and images to the project at a crucial time—when condemnation and demolition were well underway but new tenants and new visitors had not been courted in large-enough numbers. Articles in the *New York Times* and *Crane's Business Weekly* described the scale of the project and the importance of developing short- and long-term strategies for exciting and reassuring potential investors:

> The New York State Urban Development Corporation condemned about 34 buildings and moved out 236 tenants to pave the way for the project it abandoned last week. Over the next six months, the agency hopes to come up with a new plan to revive the area as a shopping, tourism and entertainment center.[19]

> State and city officials are shelving major elements of the long-delayed 42nd Street Development Project and, instead, studying short-term solutions for eliminating the sex shops and attracting retail development. . . . Officials are considering ways to keep stores operating on the sites of the four skyscrapers planned for the eastern end of the project. In the past year, the state Urban Development Corp. has cleared two of those sites of almost all of their 230 tenants. But planners now say they will not begin construction until anchor office tenants are found, which might take years in the current economic climate. Harold Holzer, a UDC executive vice president, acknowledged that planners were now considering short-term solutions. "We're examining a way to ensure the rejuvenation of 42nd Street no matter what the market," he says.[20]

Design proved to be the key to bridging the gap between Times Squares as a reality and as UDC's ideal. Hiring Stern, one of Disney's favored architects, made perfect sense. But Kalman would prove to have the greatest impact on the construction and promotion of a new image for Times Square. Using design's capacities for representation and imaging, Kalman was able to help the UDC smooth the transition from the old to the new at a time when the success of the project was still in doubt.

Kalman, one of the most famous designers of the late twentieth century, may be best known for his controversial ads for Benetton, and for editing Benetton's magazine, *Colors*. In 1989 he cochaired an American Institute of Graphic Artists conference called "Dangerous Ideas," at which he advocated for an end to wasteful product packaging and irresponsible messages in advertising. Because of this work, Kalman gained a reputation as an "entrepreneurial leftist" designer.[21]

> KURT ANDERSEN: "Do you think your involvement with planning the new 42nd Street had a big effect on what turned out?"
> TIBOR KALMAN: "I mean, personally—I want to be very sure of how I say this . . . I feel totally responsible."[22]

Kalman's claims to have been "totally responsible" for the transformation of Times Square, was part humor and part truth. He was the project's self-ascribed guru and saw this work as part of his larger professional mission:

> Returning to New York in 1997 after a three year stint as full time
> *Colors* editor in Rome and a battle with cancer, Kalman has
> re-established a leaner M&Co. with a new mission—accepting
> work only from what Kalman refers to as "non-commercial"
> clients (including the 42nd Street renewal project, which
> continues apace), Kalman's post *Colors* M&Co. has redefined its
> priorities. Gone are the "logos, brochures, motels, tomato sauce or
> corporate bullshit," says Kalman. Now he takes on only work that
> matters to him and has found a way to make commercial art serve
> society, the ultimate client.[23]

It is interesting that Kalman considered his work in Times Square to be for society and not for corporate interests,[24] particularly when his comments on the success of the project refer specifically to the kinds of tenants that chose to locate in the New Times Square:

> To me, it's amazing that Disney is now going to build two hotels
> on the corner of Eighth Avenue and 42nd Street. It's astounding.

And that something like Condé Nast would build in Times Square. So it's been an incredibly fabulous experience.[25]

Kalman's design work included everything from reimagining the way the New Times Square would eventually look from block to block to creating one-time art installations and ad campaigns during key moments in the redevelopment process. For example, Kalman codified new lighting requirements based on the energetic visual qualities of the old Times Square. He also set up a temporary sign outside of the police headquarters that read "EVERYBODY."[26]

Kalman saw one of the most important components of his role as the creation of a new image for the New Times Square. Early drawings produced by Kalman's office bear a strong resemblance to Times Square as it looks today.[27] The drawings included a cacophony of layered flashing signs, an image that must have been welcomed by the UDC at a time when most of the lights along Forty-second Street were out because the buildings had been condemned. Kalman described a sketch his office produced depicting a portion of Forty-second Street near Seventh Avenue:

> It was very much what we wanted to do. I mean, I had always had this love for vernacular, and the fundamental concept of Times Square and 42nd Street was to make 42nd Street look like it should look . . . with a lot of action on the street, with a real sense of democracy on the sidewalks. Once we had a vision, which is what those drawings represent, all we had to do was to translate those drawings into guidelines.[28]

Kalman translated the look of pre-demolition Times Square buildings and streets into guidelines for the design of new buildings on cleared parcels. He allowed the UDC to maintain the *image* of Times Square as a unique and diverse neighborhood while they dismantled and severed existing social networks and activities. The "skin" Kalman codified would make it appear as if the buildings behind all the signs were as detailed and complex as the signs they were covered with, when in fact the opposite was true (Figure 3.2). Through eminent domain, the UDC took smaller parcels from many owners and regrouped them to be sold to larger corporate interests. Because of Kalman, the New Times Square would "look" democratic.

But even after Kalman had come up with the new image for the New Times Square, it would be years before the image would become reality. Another design concept that could be implemented in a shorter time frame was needed to maintain the

Figure 3.2. Times Square construction site, 1998.

54

image until it was fulfilled. When the last of the old tenants finally left in 1996 and demolition was slated to begin, it was clear that expanses of Times Square would be covered with construction fences. Much of this reconstruction would happen along West Forty-second Street between Seventh and Eighth avenues. However, there were still porn shops and other "blighted" businesses along portions of Eighth Avenue. Seventh Avenue was a different story. The city had successfully courted corporate tenants, including MTV and Disney, and was under pressure to make sure that the image of the New Times Square was "clean, safe and friendly."[29] Design proved key to bridging the long expanses of time opened up by the eminent-domain process and to developing the impression of transformation, even before the transformation was complete.

> What happened and how it happened. New York, summer of
> 1997: plans were being finalized for the complete reconstruction
> of the entertainment district around 42nd Street, from Broadway
> west to Eighth Avenue. Tibor Kalman, in his role as architectural
> and cultural guru of the 42nd Street Development Project,
> suggested that since the whole area was about to be swathed in
> construction fences, something should be done in the spirit of
> Times Square to make the fences decorative, a form of
> entertainment in themselves. Tibor proposed that the fences be
> covered with poster-sized portraits of the denizens of Times
> Square, whomever they proved to be, as a way of giving the
> sidewalks back to the people who used them.[30]

Photographer Neil Selkirk produced 1,000 images from photos taken on a Saturday and a Tuesday in March 1998. The people who were photographed were asked for their name, where they were from, and why they had come to Times Square that day. Kalman described the people of New York as

> a unique, shifting, flowing community of the world's citizens
> who love New York: those who are curious and excited by cities,
> sidewalks, entertainment, history, architecture, democracy,
> shopping, sex, electricity, advertising, commercialism, and most of
> all, watching the antics of strangers.[31]

The day before the shoot, nervous that no one would want to have their picture taken, Kalman called a few publicists who encouraged their celebrity clients to show up with promises of having their faces printed on huge posters. As a result, Selkirk's photographs include a smattering of celebrities such as clothing designer Tommy Hilfiger and performance artists the Blue Man Group. The photographs were produced as posters that hung over the construction fences and as a collection in a book titled *1000 on 42nd Street*. In the book's afterword, Selkirk described the photography sessions and the excitement they caused:

> We set up a white backdrop in the doorway of the ruinous old Times Square Theater. In front of the backdrop we placed a simple, height-adjustable metal frame. A table was set up where the subjects would fill out the requisite permission forms, declaring name, address, and reason for being in Times Square . . . the first tentative passerby paused to see what was going on. They stepped up to the frame one by one and looked into the camera. Suddenly there was a line, then a crowd. The extraordinary thing about the whole event was the euphoria that surrounded it. There was a warmth in the air, a sense that everyone was being appreciated for being exactly whoever they were. We made no requests regarding anyone's appearance, and no one was turned away; we were unwittingly creating and participating in a celebration of just being.[32]

Selkirk's photos are beautiful. Each person was shot from the shoulders up, so their face fills the picture. The expressions range from silly to stoic. Most people are smiling. Looking at the slightly watery eyes and reddish cheeks of some of the faces—one can almost imagine what the weather was like the days of the shoot. The photos together show a group of people from a range of ethnicities and ages all shot against the same white backdrop. There is even a photo of a dog.

In the final images, a bright red button was added to everyone's shirt. On the buttons is printed each person's name, hometown, and reason for being in Times Square. Across the top of each poster the person's first name is printed in large red letters. Roman, from Brooklyn, "was walking." Eva, from Hillsborough, NJ, "came to see the construction." Carlos, from the Bronx, "was on patrol for the Guardian Angels." Lilley, from Branford, Connecticut, "was going to see *Ragtime*." The posters were hung carefully on the construction fences. They were evenly spaced and the subjects' eyes were almost at the eye level of people walking past. They appeared to be shoulder to shoulder, a sort of chorus line of faces. Amid the row in front of the soon-to-be Madame Tussaud's wax museum was a sign the same size as the posters that read "The People of 42nd Street."

But when one compares the photographs in Selkirk's book to the posters that were produced and hung on the construction fences, there are discrepancies. On some posters, the subject's reason for being in Times Square has been altered. While I have records of only six of the original posters to compare with those published in Selkirk's book, two of these have been edited. In the collection, Lisa says she is in

Figure 3.3. Lisa's portrait as published in the Selkirk collection, 2001. Her button says she is in Times Square "looking for chicks with dicks." Copyright 1998 Neil Selkirk Inc., from *1000 on 42nd Street*.

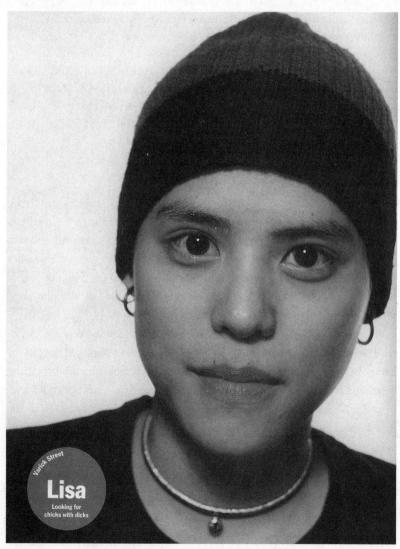

Times Square "looking for chicks with dicks" (Figure 3.3). Lisa's poster that was hung in Times Square says she is "being nice" (Figure 3.4). In the collection, Duane says he is in Times Square "looking for sex"; but his poster says he is "looking for love." Looking through the portraits in the book and reading the reasons for being in Times Square, one can almost guess who else may have undergone "motivational changes." For instance, Kelly, who was "looking at all the smut," and Adam,

Figure 3.4. Poster of Lisa on a Times Square construction fence, 1998. Her button says she is in Times Square "being nice."

CONDEMNING THE PUBLIC

who "thought there were hookers here," were most likely given more "clean, safe, and friendly" buttons. Selkirk, when interviewed in fall 2002, had no idea that these "edits" had taken place.

While it is not clear whether Kalman or the Forty-second Street Redevelopment Project were responsible for the button changes, the final effect of Kalman's campaign and its relationship to larger processes of condemnation and reconstruction are unmistakable. He covered hundreds of feet of construction fence with huge posters of smiling people. Those people's desires were edited to create the morality of the New Times Square. Their ranks included a smattering of stars. This public body (albeit two-dimensional) represented and advertised the new public for the New Times Square even before this public had appeared on the scene. Graphic design was used to transform the public: specifically, its intentions and actions in public space. Kalman's impulse to make "poster-sized portraits of the denizens of Times Square, whomever they proved to be, as a way of giving the sidewalks back to the people who used them" was inclusive in intention but exclusive in practice. To be part of the group, one had to conform, or, rather, one had to be reformed. The act of editing was not done by the people themselves, but by the designer of the campaign. The campaign was reassuring. It indicated that the transformation of the neighborhood was progressing. New buildings were under construction and new people had arrived on the scene. It verified that the process set in motion by the UDC was working. Demolition *would* lead to regeneration of the right kind of urban setting for the right kind of urban public.

Kalman's work in Times Square supported and promoted larger economic and political processes. As Kalman himself wrote, "In focusing on its artistic and formal qualities, history has neglected the graphic design's role as a medium—each artifact marks more than a place in the progression of artistic sensibility. Each also speaks eloquently of its social history. All you have to do is learn the language."[33] The "language" of Kalman's work is contradictory. It appears inclusive and egalitarian. However, setting appropriate reasons for being in a public space is a way of justifying exclusion. If you are not in Times Square to see a show, why are you there? If you are not in Times Square to shop, why are you there? Constructing a public with appropriate desires and activities, printing their faces on huge posters and hanging them on the "walls" of a public space is a material way of marking out a social territory.

The posters were of individuals but were produced and presented as a public body. Together they formed a kind of whole, an "e pluribus unum" (of the many, we are one): a statement found on every U.S. coin. Although

**60**

the faces are different and the motivations are different, all the photography subjects fall within a prescribed set. They are part of the same group because they were photographed during the same two-day period in the same location. Whether or not they are "the public" of Times Square is debatable. As a set of individual objects, the posters indicate that if publics can be assembled, they can be disassembled. The posters also "covered-up" the physical editing of the neighborhood by distracting attention from the demolition that happened behind them—literally masking the processes of destruction and reconstruction.

The "moral" overhaul that the posters underwent becomes even more troubling in light of the new morality of the New Times Square. The Dangerous Deuce was not transformed into a family-friendly pseudo-environment. The New Times Square contains exploitative images of women and narratives that condone violence.[34] New billboard ads capitalize on the "tawdry" image of the old Times Square, as even a brief sampling of advertisements shows. For example, a Buffalo Jeans advertisement photographed in 2001 bears a striking resemblance to a photograph of a blow-up doll in a pornography shop window taken in 1984 (Figure 3.5, Figure 3.6). A Puma advertisement featuring Pamela Lee also indicates that women's bodies are still currency in Times Square (Figure 3.7).

Kalman himself was disappointed with the ads and signs in the New Times Square, but for very different reasons. In a *Metropolis Magazine* interview in 1998, Kalman emphasized the importance of design to the success of the New Times Square, specifically the emphasis on bright lights and lots of advertising. But, he added, "I think the street looks like hell now. . . . Everything is brand-new. It's like a new pair of jeans—stiff and awkward, with everybody just trying to follow the rules. But they will break in with time. The market will create the proper cacophony by itself."[35] Kalman was right in saying that "the market" would continue to "create" Times Square, but completely wrong about the implications. Instead of "breaking in," the New Times Square constantly renews itself with new billboards and advertising "spectaculars" (Figure 3.8). It seems outrageous that someone as corporate savvy as Kalman would imagine that companies in Times Square that spend larger and larger portions of their budgets on brand creation and maintenance would ever allow their public faces to "break in." In fact, the diodes on the Panasonic LED screen are checked nightly to make sure that the image is perfect.

Advertising in Times Square is so costly because it reaches the millions of tourists and the odd New Yorkers who bother to look up, as well as

Figure 3.5. Photograph of a Times Square
sex business on Forty-second Street
taken in 1984 by the UDC. Courtesy of
the Forty-second Street Development
Project, Inc.

Figure 3.6. An advertisement for Buffalo
Jeans in the New Times Square, 2000.

Figure 3.7. An advertisement
for Puma running shoes
featuring Pamela Anderson,
2000.

the worldwide audiences of networks like MTV, ABC, and CBS. It's also hard to imagine cacophonies erupting in the New Times Square, where megacorporations overlay the geography of streets. Times Square Studios, home to ABC's *Good Morning America* and episodes of *20/20*, is owned by Disney. Disney also owns ABC. The sports bar ESPN Zone is named after the popular cable television station also owned by Disney. Across Broadway from the Times Square Studios is the studio for MTV. Around the corner from MTV on Forty-second Street is a huge set of billboards for CBS. Both MTV and CBS are owned by Viacom, one of the major owners of Times Square outdoor advertising space. The content showed on the giant Panasonic screen is fed from CNBC, which is co-owned by NBC and Microsoft.

Kalman was wrong when he said that time and the market would bring about a looser, more vibrant social life in Times Square (or even a convincing visual image of one). The "invisible hand" of the market, as guided by the UDC, has instead spurred new rounds of condemnation, eviction, demolition, parcel consolidation, and reconstruction in New York and in other cities in the United States.[36] One of the most vocal boosters of the Times Square model was former New York Governor George E. Pataki. Touting the "rebirth" of Times Square as a model for urban redevelopment, Pataki toured Forty-second Street in May 2001 with the governors of Connecticut, Michigan, and Pennsylvania. During the tour, Pataki invited the three governors

Figure 3.8. A Times Square "spectacular" billboard, 2002.

to "come back with their families to enjoy the excitement that is the new New York."[37]

The Times Square story, whether you view it as a triumph or a tragedy, is unquestionably one of transformation. Geographers and sociologists have written about the politics that drove the transformation.[38] Architects have lamented the "Disneyfication" of the resulting image. Legal scholars have argued about the use of eminent domain to transfer property from one set of private hands to another. But the ways in which the transformation was contingent upon design practices has not been explored. At Federal Plaza, design was used to create a new physical environment that supported only a very specific set of uses tied to a particular idea of what public space and public life should be. While design in Times Square resulted in a physical transformation, design practices occurring throughout the redevelopment process proved crucial. A poster campaign is not the same as a plaza redesign. But it is a potent way of marking appropriate public bodies and promoting appropriate public activities.

Ironically, renewal projects patterned after the "success" of Times Square happened *in Times Square.* Just months after Pataki invited other governors to return to the area with their families, the UDC argued in court that the blocks immediately adjacent to Times Square were home to "an active drug trade," "blight," and, "low-end retail and food establishments"[39] and therefore the properties should be condemned and demolished to make way for a headquarters for the *New York Times*. Property owners argued that these claims were untrue, that any "blight" in Times Square was gone, and that any remaining economic problems could be blamed on the UDC for holding the threat of condemnation over the heads of property owners who might have otherwise invested in their buildings and businesses.

The same year that Pataki toured Times Square with visiting governors and that condemnations for the new *New York Times* tower began, Michael Sorkin published his book *Some Assembly Required*. In a chapter titled "Times Square: Status Quo Vadis," Sorkin writes, "it is terribly true that the demise of Times Square, its conversion to another version of the recursion of Vegas . . . must be blamed squarely not simply on the energetic advocates of sanitized fun but on our own failures to propose a better idea."[40]

What designers can imagine and promote depends on what they believe "counts" as design and what they believe needs to be changed. However, even if designers proposed better ideas for Times Square, significant political and economic barriers to their implementation would remain. Therefore, how much blame can comfortably rest on the shoulders of a designer like Kalman? Conversely, should Kalman only be faulted with a "lack of imagination"? Perhaps we can only blame Kalman for being either too naive, too self-delusional, or too insincere to realize that he was doing anything but creating a Times Square–like skin for what amounts to a large-scale, state-brokered, taxpayer-funded corporate takeover of a portion of midtown Manhattan. Kalman's work at Times Square is even harder to swallow because he set himself up as a socially minded leftist graphic designer.[41] In this particular project, Kalman provided aesthetic fixes for the problems encountered by the UDC in the redevelopment process:

> Got huge expanses of fence because you condemned an entire neighborhood? Not a lot of people around because most of them were chucked out of their stores, homes, and theaters? Put faces on posters.
>
> Worried your new Times Square will look sterile and monolithic? Break up the monotony with some colorful signs.

While this chapter addresses very different parts of the redevelopment process, from the initial condemnation to the experience of being in Times Square today, understanding the limits and powers of design is central to building models for more "democratic" approaches to urban redevelopment and to imaging the role of the designer in these approaches. An examination of the legal structure of eminent domain is particularly timely. In June 2005 the U.S. Supreme Court decided on a case filed on behalf of New London, Connecticut, homeowners whose houses were up for condemnation to make way for an office complex, parking lot, and park that would primarily bene- fit the pharmaceutical company, Pfizer. The court ruled in favor of the city of New London, arguing that "[t]he city's proposed disposition of petition- ers' property qualifies as a public use within the meaning of the Takings Clause." The court upheld New London's argument that the city had the right to take the property because "the area at issue was sufficiently dis- tressed to justify a program of economic rejuvenation."[42]

Even this new ruling, which limits the right of property owners to fight against eminent domain, upholds property owners' right to financial compen- sation. The ruling highlights the fact that while property owners have the right to financial recourse, the rest of us—tenants, workers, patrons, passersby— have none. While building owners may take their money and go elsewhere and have rights to timely compensation, everyone else just has to go. This is not to say that the law ignores them. In Times Square, the existing pub- lic was legally defined as the problem: something to be removed. To many Times Square visitors today, it would seem that the removal has "worked." Based on conversations with friends and family, middle-class people cer- tainly feel safer in Times Square today. But is Times Square safer as a *result* of the process of redevelopment? Do middle-class white people feel safer in Times Square simply because there are more people like them there now?

It is also difficult to prove that any decrease in crime in Times Square is a result of the specific approach to development taken there: condem- nation, parcel aggregation, and the creation of large corporate office spaces and franchise retail spaces. As mentioned, the city was never able to make a convincing argument that there was a correlation between crime and porn shops. Also, if we argue that Times Square is a much safer place to live, work, shop, and relax after redevelopment, have the people who used to work, shop, and relax in Times Square in the 1970s and 1980s benefited from this change? For example, is life better for the children, men, and women who were sex workers in Times Square? Odds are the answer is no. Sex workers who used to work in Times Square moved to other areas of the city. Their safety at work was not helped by the change in Times Square. Making their work safer has little to do with the physical places they work in and everything to do with their working conditions and whether they have access to health care. Because the sex industry isn't headquartered in Times Square anymore doesn't mean that it has left the city. Most of the intensive sex trade has moved out of Manhattan to neighboring areas such as Red Hook in Queens.

So what should have happened in Times Square? First of all, the city should have worked with existing residents and existing building owners and nearby Hell's Kitchen residents to come up with a set of goals for what Times Square needed to become. If the city's and the state's main concerns were health, morality, and safety, as they argued in the eminent-domain proceedings, they should have started by asking how they could improve the health of the people who lived and worked in Times Square. The results would, I think, have been very different, and perhaps, from an urban design standpoint, boring and invisible. Perhaps it would have included more Single Room Occupancy Housing (instead of a reduction). Perhaps it would have included safe spaces for sex workers to bring customers. Perhaps there would have been treatment centers and job training. Perhaps they would have increased the number of police in the area, or used state money to help building owners convert their buildings into office space, live-work units, schools, or hotels.

Who knows what possibilities there were and what might have come out of a redevelopment process not driven by money and political alliances. It's not up to designers to make these kinds of decisions either. The kind of imagining that Sorkin calls for (and I think he would agree) should have happened in concert with local community boards and neighborhood organizations in Times Square, Hell's Kitchen, and Clinton.

What if Kalman had refused the job (and a famous designer like him is in a much better position to do so than most) and instead decided to offer his services to neighboring districts? What if he had challenged the city to spend as much money in Clinton as it had in Times Square, but for the benefit of *existing* residents, workers, and property owners? Could his skills in imagining, representing, and promoting values and ideas through design have helped support the work of community groups?

While we must imagine alternatives to the Times Square redevelopment process, as Sorkin argues we should, we must also understand the power of the legal processes of urban design. We must be prepared to challenge plans that claim to be in the public's interest by examining these projects and their moral claims. We must recognize the power of design to promote such plans by making places that look public, that look like they reflect multiple viewpoints, but are simply creating veneers.

The Times Square case reveals, perhaps in hyperbolic fashion, what is at stake in design and how effective combinations of moral, legal, and design arguments can be. Moral and economic arguments justify the erasure of publics, laws enforce the "right" of the state to condemn and demolish, and design eases the shock of the physical dismantling with instant physical forms that prefigure the full transformation.

Our imagined alternatives must therefore be accompanied by strategies for challenging the moral and economic arguments put forth by what are often, but not exclusively, state-corporate teams. We must find the points in the process (legislative, judicial) at which specific criticisms might stop or at least stall the layers of required approvals. We must recognize the differences between impressions of democracy and democratic practices. In the absence of these discussions, landscape architects, architects, interior designers, graphic designers, public artists, and urban designers may concretize—in built form, aesthetic representations, and programmatic systems—restrictive definitions of the public and public space.

# 4 Bamboozled? Access, Ownership, and the IBM Atrium

> At dusk . . . the snow glistened on the slanted glass
> panes of the saw-toothed roof above the towering
> bamboo trees in the new IBM Garden Plaza. . . .
> Sheltered and comfortable within, one could observe
> the cold, gleaming streets and the moving lights of
> traffic without—a nineteenth-century winter garden
> revived in modern form.
> —Paula Deitz, "Design Notebook," New
> York Times, March 3, 1983

> Why I was foolish enough to believe that a real estate
> developer and a commercial gallery would act in a
> selfless, altruistic manner for the people of New York
> City is beyond me.
> —Member of Community Board Five

**The final three chapters** examine three of New York's nearly 530 POPS: the former IBM Atrium, Sony Plaza, and the public spaces of Trump Tower (Figure 4.1). POPS are developed under the Plaza Bonus Zoning Ordinance. First enacted in 1961, and revised in 1975 and 1999, the ordinance allows developers to construct additional building floors if they provide a POPS inside or next to their building. Each POPS is governed by an individual contract between the building owner and the city. The contracts state the size and attributes of the POPS and how many additional floors the owner is allowed to build as a result. The building and the public space are legally privately owned, but the owner gives up the right to exclude members of the public. The Department of City Planning must review any changes that a POPS owner proposes to make to the spaces. If a building changes hands, the new owner is bound by the original contract. POPS, as physical spaces and legal entities, are the result of complex relationships between local government agencies, private corporations, and the public.

POPS have received greater attention in the last five years, in part due to a book titled *Privately Owned Public Space: The New York City Experience*, written by Jerold Kayden, the New York City Department of City Planning,

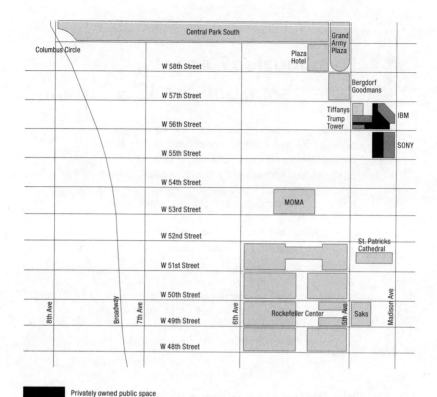

Central Park South

Columbus Circle

Plaza Hotel

Grand Army Plaza

W 58th Street

Bergdorf Goodmans

W 57th Street

Tiffanys
Trump Tower

IBM

W 56th Street

SONY

W 55th Street

W 54th Street

MOMA

W 53rd Street

W 52nd Street

St. Patricks Cathedral

W 51st Street

W 50th Street

8th Ave

Broadway

7th Ave

6th Ave

Rockefeller Center

5th Ave

Saks

Madison Ave

W 49th Street

W 48th Street

Privately owned public space

Figure 4.1. Location map for Privately Owned Public Spaces. Drafted by Vincent deBritto.

and the Municipal Art Society of New York. The book is a part of a larger project to document POPS contracts and to establish exactly what "kind" of public space each developer was meant to provide—down to the number of tables and chairs, opening hours, garbage receptacles, etc. This was no small task. The team found POPS that had been converted into parking areas, subsumed completely by private retail uses, or simply locked. As a result of their work, more POPS have been brought into compliance. The authors argued that the Department of City Planning lacks funding to ensure that all POPS are in constant compliance.

The next three chapters show that problems with the POPS program run deeper than building owners not living up to their contracts. Even POPS that are in full compliance—those that are the best the program has to offer— reveal fundamental problems with the POPS program. Such problems are inherent in the very idea of a "privately owned public space" and to failures of New York's program in particular. At the POPS program's core is the assumption that corporations can provide what local governments are no longer funded to do: in this case, building and managing publicly funded public spaces. As Kayden notes, members of the public are "de facto third-party beneficiaries." They gain the right to enter and use this private property, but "endure whatever extra congestion and loss of light and air that may result from the grant of extra floor area or other regulatory concessions."[1] But the problems with POPS as public spaces go beyond trade-offs for light and air. This chapter, for example, discusses the controversy over proposed changes to the IBM Atrium. The IBM case shows that POPS contracts—which were developed to protect public interests—instead severely limit the possibility for these spaces to ever be dynamically public. Ties between POPS and public spheres that might develop around them are institutionally precluded. The POPS program frames the public as people with physical access but no political access.

When IBM consolidated its office holdings in the early 1990s, it sold the office tower, and by default the atrium, to real estate mogul Edward Minskoff. In 1994 Minskoff proposed to transform the atrium into an art exhibition space. This proposal prompted one of the biggest controversies over a privately owned public space in New York. Opposition to changing the atrium was strong because the atrium was, by many accounts, one of the most beautiful public spaces in New York.

The atrium first opened to the public in 1983 and consistently received glowing reviews from architecture critics, arts organizations, and visitors. It was called "exuberant," "elegant," an "oasis," and "a tree-filled conservatory and public living room rolled into one."[2] Architect Edward Larrabee Barnes designed the IBM Building, and landscape architects Robert Zion and Harold Breen collaborated with Barnes on the design of the atrium. Their scheme for the atrium was quite simple: a greenhouse-like structure with eleven stands of bamboo reaching up to the sixty-five-foot-tall ceilings, with tables and movable chairs below (Figure 4.2). A 1991 article, "Strolling Hidden Nooks in Manhattan's Canyons," described the atrium as part of a "Northwest Passage through the skyscraper wilderness." The article proposed an itinerary through "cloisters away from the city's unrelenting throb." The itinerary began at the atrium: "Start elegantly at IBM's glass-canopied public thoroughfare . . . stroll through a lush public garden of bamboo and pink flowers where idlers read newspapers and drink coffee in a scene evocative of Europe."[3] Bamboo has an intense, almost lime-green color. One can imagine the contrast of this color against the wet, dark-black streets and the

BAMBOOZLED?

red and green of the traffic lights, headlights, and brake lights outside, and how quiet the space was in contrast to the din of Manhattan rush hour. The Municipal Art Society[4] declared that the IBM Atrium was "universally lauded as the finest bonused indoor public space in New York City and most successful melding of social and aesthetic amenities ever produced by incentive zoning."[5]

While the IBM Atrium may be the most successful result of the POPS program, ironically its design and its most outstanding qualities had nothing to do with the program. The atrium fulfilled almost all of the planning department's new regulations for POPS. It had movable chairs, a food kiosk, entrances at street level, and clear views in and out of the space. However, these are only a few aspects of what made the space "magical." Nowhere in the contract with IBM did the planning department specify that there should be a grove of bamboo trees that canopied the space. Nor did it require that the atrium be made almost entirely of glass, so that in the evening, visitors could look up at the lights in nearby office buildings. This is not to say that the design was accidental. IBM chose one of the most respected architectural and landscape architectural firms to design the atrium. Edward Larrabee Barnes designed the atrium in collaboration with the landscape architecture firm of Zion and Breen. Zion and Breen are perhaps best known for Paley Park, regarded as the best small park in Manhattan, and widely imitated.[6]

The atrium was unique in the city, and perhaps in the country, because of its twelve stands of towering bright green bamboo. The removal of even a few of the stands of bamboo would therefore destroy the unique tranquility of the space. Opponents to Minskoff's plans to transform the atrium into an art exhibition space argued that he was bringing a corporate venture into a public space. In the end, a compromise was struck. Only three of eleven stands of bamboo would be removed, and more seating would be added. But the impact on the atrium was substantial. What was once a thick grove became a few stands. The light entering the atrium, no longer filtered by layers of leaves, gave the space a washed-out gray look, or, as one commentator noted, "[o]n a recent spring day, with the outdoors brisk and the sky bright blue, a visitor to the sculpture garden was greeted instead with a pale wintry environment, as if Snow White had just bitten into the Queen's bad apple."[7] Instead of providing a sense of intimacy, greenness, and enclosure, the new atrium was stark and exposed (Figure 4.3).

Minskoff's renovation went ahead without a public hearing. Even though the proposed changes

Figure 4.2. Original IBM Atrium, 1992. Courtesy of Dianne Harris.

Figure 4.3. Atrium after renovation, 2001.

would completely alter the atrium, according to the legal structure of the POPS program and decisions made by the Department of City Planning, there was no way for people who used the atrium to block Minskoff's proposal. For this reason, the atrium stopped being a dynamically public space before the bamboo came down. It was never public because, from its inception, decisions over how it would be managed over time were out of the hands of the public. Access is a matter of ongoing input into processes of change and maintenance. Put differently, physical access is of course crucial to public spaces being public. But equally important is access to and agency within the processes that govern public spaces.

The IBM Atrium was a wonderfully designed public space. The story of the atrium reveals the insufficiency of the legal structure of the POPS program to protect well-designed spaces. However, the story also shows that the program has almost no legal provisions for ongoing participation of those outside government and business in the processes that change these sites. Arguably, the atrium would never have been changed if the decision-making process were set up to address public concerns as strongly as it protects private concerns.

This chapter relies on archival materials, including letters of complaint to the Department of City Planning, articles in local newspapers, correspondence between the building owner and the Department of City Planning,

BAMBOOZLED?

and planning department reports to explore these issues. These documents, and, interestingly, the process of gaining access to them, show that public involvement in POPS is institutionally absent. The legal structure governing the ongoing management of these spaces prevents those people who use the spaces from knowing about and having a say in physical and programmatic changes to those spaces.

## The Original Contract and the Original Design

Architectural critic Herbert Muschamp said, "With its tall, airy bamboo stalks set off by walls of charcoal granite, the atrium of the IBM Building . . . resembles a cross between a public park and a corporate lobby." Muschamp's description of the former IBM Atrium as a cross between a park and a lobby referred to more than the atrium's appearance. POPS are the material result of a legal agreement between the city and private building owners. While the IBM Atrium does not contain all the functions of a corporate lobby (its switchboard and elevator area are separated from the atrium by a glass wall), the lobby is attached to the building physically, legally, and economically. Its hybrid appearance, part corporate and part public, bespeaks the complex contract that generated its form and function. The contract between IBM and the city was individually negotiated prior to the building's construction and according to standards set out in the Plaza Bonus Zoning Ordinance. In return for constructing and maintaining the atrium and a plaza in front of the building,[8] IBM was able to build an additional 147,600 square feet of office space.[9] The exact value of this bonus is difficult to determine. A 1982 *New York Times* article noted that rents in prime locations such as midtown and the financial district ran between $30 to $40 per square foot, per year. The square footage in this case could have meant an extra $5,166,000 in annual rental revenues for IBM.

But a comparison of what is actually called for in the contract between IBM and the Department of City Planning under the POPS program shows that to a great degree the success of the initial atrium design had little to do with legal leverage and everything to do with thoughtful design. This thoughtfulness was not just about the inclusion of the bamboo grove. It also related to large-scale design decisions about the relationships between the private spaces of the corporate tower and the public spaces of the atrium.

IBM hired two excellent designers to develop the public spaces. As a result, the atrium's configuration, from the large to the small scale, worked as a public space in ways that most other POPS developed at the same time and according to the same standards did not. Muschamp hit on one of these points when he described it as a park and a lobby, but he didn't note the ways the corporate and the public spaces are fairly separate. At the scale of the entire building, there is a clearer distinction between the private spaces of the corporate tower and the public spaces of the atrium. The atrium is not embedded deep within a private building—as is the case, for example, at the Citicorp Building a few blocks away.

The distinction between the atrium and the office tower is clearly distinguishable by passersby at ground level. The building's footprint is complicated. It is not a simple slab. It does not fill its lot. Nor is it pulled back from the sidewalk evenly. It can be seen as two buildings: an office tower and a greenhouse (Figure 4.4). The two nest against each other as more or less triangular portions of the same square. Tips of each triangle are cut off to create entrance plazas. What is interesting about the public spaces, particularly the atrium,

Figure 4.4. Exterior of atrium, 2001.

is the degree to which they stand on their own. The atrium is clearly attached to the office tower, but only along one wall. The southern wall faces onto the sidewalk of Fifty-sixth Street. The southwestern wall is an interior wall with a connection to the public spaces of Trump Tower. The northeastern wall is a clear glass wall with doors through to the lobby of the office tower. And the eastern wall, the shortest of the walls, is glass, and leads out into the public plaza on Madison Avenue. The roof to the atrium is also glass, reinforcing the feeling that it is almost its own structure. The IBM Atrium's tranquility, at least the auditory tranquility, comes from being physically separated from the sidewalk and street by glass walls. These transparent walls serve to privilege the atrium's proximity and relationship to the outside over and against its relationship to the indoor lobby on the other side of the atrium (Figure 4.5).

Again, this independence was not a requirement of the contract with the Department of City Planning. The separation of atrium and office tower at the IBM building is very different from interior public spaces in adjacent midtown high rises. For example, Trump Tower completely envelops the public spaces within the building. Some have argued they are almost indistinguishable as public spaces at all. The Sony Atrium, visible from IBM across Fifty-sixth Street, borders office and retail spaces along two of its four walls—and these are the longest two. The atrium at Citicorp is not only embedded inside the building but is sunken below street level. Because of its visual openness to the street and the sky and the clear distinction between office tower and atrium greenhouse, the IBM Atrium has a much stronger sense of being a freely accessible space.

Zion and Breen consulted William H. Whyte on the design of the atrium. Whyte was the public-space guru of Manhattan, the author of revisions to the POPS program in 1975, and a relentless activist for more and better public spaces. His influence on the design of the atrium is clear. The atrium seemed to be the physical manifestation of Whyte's public space ideals as published in his *The Social Life of Small Urban Spaces*. The atrium is clearly visible to and from the street on the sides bordering East Fifty-ninth Street and Madison Avenue. Glass walls rise four stories to the atrium ceiling, which is topped with serrated trusses.[10] When it was first constructed, eleven stands of bamboo divided the atrium into smaller spaces and filtered the light as it fell to the granite floor. Giant concrete dishes of flowers were changed seasonally and added color to the otherwise gray and green space, which included a food kiosk, at-grade entrances, clear visibility between the inside and outside, and movable chairs.

The most memorable feature of the original atrium was the grove of bamboo. No other public space in Manhattan had such a garden. The bamboo helped divide the 10,000-square-foot atrium into smaller seating areas. It muffled noises that would have otherwise echoed off the granite and glass. Eventually, the bamboo became home to birds that fed off crumbs left by noontime lunchers. The birds' twittering and rustling was audible because the space was protected from the noise of the streets outside. William Whyte was fond of the space, and returned periodically to observe how people were using it. One thing Whyte noticed during these observations was that people would move atrium chairs (the tables were fixed at this time) to sit at the base of the bamboo trees. This behavior supported the findings of his earlier studies that showed how people preferred seating that had something behind it: a wall, a tree, etc. The bamboo

Figure 4.5. Plan view of atrium within building. Drafted by Vincent deBritto. Courtesy of New York Department of City Planning.

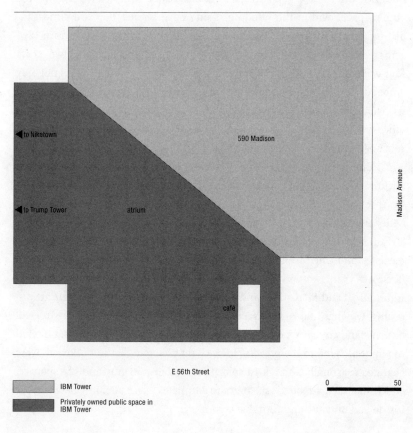

E 57th Street

to Niketown

590 Madison

to Trump Tower

atrium

Madison Avneue

café

E 56th Street

0      50

IBM Tower

Privately owned public space in IBM Tower

grove also served to separate the seating area of the atrium from the walkway area. The walkway provided an interior connection between Fifty-sixth
and Fifty-seventh streets. The seating area was visible from the walkway, but
it was clearly a distinct area. It didn't become apparent exactly how well loved
the atrium and its lush grove of bamboo were until proposals were made by
a new building owner to alter the space's design.

## New Owner, New Agenda

Privately owned public spaces remain public even when a building is sold
to a new owner. New owners are able to change an existing public space as
long as the changes do not come in conflict with the original contract. The
early years of IBM's ownership of the building coincided with a peak in IBM
revenues. In 1984, earnings were $6.6 billion. Not surprisingly, IBM's sale
of the building about ten years later to a New York City real estate company
coincided with one of its biggest revenue downturns. During the five years
prior to the sale, IBM had cut thousands of jobs, and in 1991 it reported a
net loss of $2.8 billion. Developer Edward Minskoff, in a joint venture with
Odyssey Partners investment group, purchased 590 Madison Avenue from
IBM in 1994 for $200 million. In 1995, during a dip in the office rental
market, Minskoff was still able to rent space in the building for about $45
per square foot, per year. The year before, rent had been closer to $50 per
square foot.

When the building changed hands, the atrium was almost exactly as
it had been initially built, despite some reports that IBM had not been maintaining the space at as high a level as it once had.[11] One year after purchas-
ing the building from IBM, Edward Minskoff applied to the Department of
City Planning to make alterations to the atrium so that he could install a
rotating exhibition of contemporary sculpture. Minskoff would manage the
exhibitions jointly with PaceWildenstein, a commercial art gallery. Minskoff
proposed removing almost all the bamboo, changing the movable chairs
and tables to benches, and hiring security guards to protect the artwork.
Minskoff's application for changes to the atrium set off a controversy that
involved the art community, realtors, designers, and commercial galleries.
Despite the controversy's high public profile, it highlighted the fragility of
government-guaranteed public space.

When Minskoff's plans were released in early 1995, the eight-month
battle over the future of the atrium began. Not surprisingly, two camps

emerged: those in favor of the sculpture garden and those against destroying the bamboo grove.[12] The first group—let's call them the pro-art group—lobbied the Department of City Planning with letters detailing the benefits of having works of art in public places. All the letters in the planning-department file that favored the original Minskoff proposal were from people who were in one way or another tied either to nonprofit or for-profit art groups. Minskoff was himself a noted art collector. In November 1996 at an auction at Christie's, Minskoff sold for $772,500 a silk-screen painting by Robert Rauschenberg titled *Shortstop*. The painting was estimated to be worth between $800,000 and $1.2 million.

The fact that a major real estate developer was also involved in collecting and selling fine art, and therefore wanted to show it in his building, is not all that shocking. Nor is the fact that the pro-art letters were from people in the art business. What is interesting is the way in which Minskoff and the pro-art camp argued that the renovation of the atrium was actually in the public's interest. A very short letter from Ivan C. Karp of OK Harris, one of the oldest commercial art galleries in SoHo, called the existing atrium "rather stark" and cited the "paucity of public evidence of the vast resources of fine art in this city."[13]

Diana D. Brooks, then president and chief executive officer of Sotheby's, wrote: "this project would be a unique opportunity to heighten cultural awareness through the public display of art work. Additionally, the creation of a sculpture garden in the IBM Atrium takes on added significance due to the diminishing federal support of the arts and the lack of funding available for any project of the same scale. It would be a shame to deny so many New Yorkers an occasion to enrich their lives through aesthetic appreciation. The appeal of New York City depends in great part on the richness and availability of the visual arts to the general public."[14] Brooks's quote asserts that the lives of the people who use the space would be unconditionally enriched by the display of art. She implies that there is a dearth of art on display in New York City. She also implies that the public's awareness of culture needs to be heightened. It is hard to accept the recommendations of the director of Sotheby's as representative of "so many New Yorkers," and I don't think this was her intention. The assumption embedded in her words is that, as a cultural leader, the art world needs to provide culture for the consumption of the masses. She also argued that because the federal government has cut funding for the arts, public space programs should help take up the slack.

BAMBOOZLED?

Those against the initial proposal included William Whyte, who was consulted by the Planning Committee in the course of their review of Minskoff's plan. In the Planning Committee report, Whyte called Minskoff's plan "retrogressive" because of the removal of the bamboo and also because of the removal of amenities like the food kiosk and the change from movable to fixed seating. The committee report also stated that the proposed space was not a sculpture garden but a sculpture gallery. They argued that the difference between the two was in the gallery's "total subjugation of the space's verdant and inviting qualities"[15] in order to make room for large-scale sculpture.

The Parks Council also argued that none of the bamboo should be removed. In a letter sent to the City Planning Commission prior to their final vote on the proposal, the Parks Council argued that "the original special permit issued by the City Planning Commission described the space as an 'enclosed sky-lit landscaped park.' In other words, from its inception this was intended to provide an interior garden respite in midtown . . . the unusual qualities of the bamboo plants have come to be uniquely identified with the atrium over the years."[16] They suggested that all the bamboo be retained and that artwork be added to the existing configuration. They noted that "keeping all the trees may mean that certain very large sculptures could not be exhibited, but this seems a small price to pay for holding on to one of the success stories of the bonus plaza program."[17]

A statement from the Municipal Art Society (MAS) on September 14, 1995, came to the same conclusion and added some additional items for consideration. It noted that during the review process regarding the atrium, Minskoff had argued that the presence of sculpture would increase public use of the space. MAS argued that while this might be the case, there were other factors that needed to be addressed. They noted that the atrium was too hot in the summer because IBM wasn't running the air conditioning, that there were no services other than the food kiosk to draw people to the space, and that the western corridor was temporarily closed because of the construction of Niketown. "Each of these conditions contributes to a temporary decline in visitors," they concluded, "not the design which indeed has enjoyed many years of success and heavy usage."[18]

As a result of the review process, Minskoff came back to the Department of City Planning with an alternate proposal. The new proposal removed three of the eleven bamboo stands and retained most of the original movable seating. The proposal was approved, and the sculpture garden opened

December 14, 1995. Marc Glimcher of PaceWildenstein Gallery remarked that the sculpture garden was "great public relations in the long-term sense. Many of these works have been sitting in warehouses, so it's wonderful that the public has the chance to enjoy them. It's also important to stress the education component here. Educating the public is the very foundation of the art market."[19] This quotation must have confirmed the fears of members of Community Board Five and others who cautioned against allowing a commercial art gallery to use a public atrium to display artwork. In order to try to prevent PaceWildenstein from benefiting directly from their involvement, the city made a stipulation that none of the artwork shown in the atrium could be for sale at the time of exhibition. Also, the city told Minskoff that he had to set up a committee that would decide curatorial matters, and that not all the exhibitions could be organized by PaceWildenstein or include artists that PaceWildenstein represented.

Statements from the planning department emphasized that the outcome of the process of review was, in the end, positive. City Planning Commissioner James B. Rose said, "This is a very good thing for the city. . . . Only three trees came down, and there's more seating than there was before." This sentiment was not, however, widely held. In "Requiem for an Atrium," Ken Smith of the Project for Public Spaces said, "The once powerful ambient effect of the bamboo garden is now gone, as is most of the magic the space once had. The altered atrium, even with the addition of colorful sculpture, is a pathetic alternative to the original, and a sad loss of public space in New York City."[20] The bamboo that is left does not give the sense of being a grove. The seating areas bleed into one another. The sense of being in an intimate canopied place is lost. The summer sunlight that was once filtered now gives the atrium a kind of gray pallor. One has less a feeling of enclosure and more a feeling of exposure. In short, the most beloved POPS—lauded by design critics, journalists, the Department of City Planning, public-space scholars, and the people who used it everyday—was transformed into something that none of them had asked for and in a way that completely destroyed its initial qualities. How was this possible?

The destruction of the atrium was possible because of the legal structure of the POPS program. The review process that allowed Minskoff to make the changes is still in place today. According to the POPS legal structure, owners may make changes to bonus spaces. There are two basic categories of changes, each with a different review process. "Major" changes require a Uniform Land Use Review Procedure (ULURP).[21] The process ends with a review by the City Planning Commission, and may also involve a review by the City Council. It does not specifically call for a public hearing but does involve elected officials who, theoretically, could be voted out in the next election if their constituents disagree with their actions. "Minor" changes need to be reviewed only by the City Planning Commission. The City Planning Commission may act in consultation with the local community board,[22] but it is not required by law. Community boards in New York City represent not only the residents of that community but also the businesses and tourists.

City Planning Commission staff members have confirmed that the difference between a major and minor change is not laid out in the zoning code. Rather, major versus minor is thought to be "intuitive and obvious." Those exact words were used in an interview with a planning department staff member. The example the staff member gave was that if the overall square footage of the space doesn't change, it is not a major renovation. In cases in which the difference between major and minor is not intuitive, Department of City Planning counsel is consulted.[23] The controversy over the renovation at IBM and the final compromise reached between Minskoff and the planning department show how even minor changes can have major effects.

Why does a public program to provide public spaces pay little or no attention to the idea of public involvement in decision making? First, when the code was initially written in 1961, it was not to provide new public spaces. Rather, the initial policy's sole stated purpose was to bring more light and air into the city. The policy was altered in 1975, but only to require amenities like seating, food concessions, and on-grade connections to the street. Second, while these alterations to the policy regarding amenities were carefully spelled out, and indeed spelled out on signs in each space and on the Department of City Planning Web site, there is little or no information in the current policy regarding who has the ability to dictate or enforce rules for conduct in the spaces or to conduct or block alterations to the space that fall outside what is spelled out in the contract. In other words, the bonus program as it is legally written and therefore enforced by the Department of City Planning focuses on providing a specific set of physical amenities. The assumption is that if these amenities are provided, the resulting spaces are public spaces. The policy does not detail who has the ability to control physical access to a space or who has access to decision-making processes. As de facto third parties in the contract, members of the public are legally guaranteed, for example, a certain amount of seating, the presence or absence of a food kiosk, and specific opening hours.

However, building owners are not all in compliance regarding the provision of required amenities. Contract enforcement has proved to be difficult. Owners limit opening hours, do not provide the correct amount of seating, and allow cafés and other private businesses to encroach on atriums and plazas. The authors of *Privately Owned Public Space* argue that the main problem with the program is the lack of enforcement of contracts. Their prescription for better enforcement, seen in light of the IBM controversy, also indicates a fundamental problem with the entire basis of New York's program: the authors argue that if the public took more of a proprietary interest in POPS, they would take an interest in helping the Department of City Planning hold owners to their contracts. The authors assert:

> [a]n effective enforcement program consists of five elements:
> up to date documentation, broad public knowledge, periodic
> inspections, meaningful remedies, and promotion of public use. . . .
> With quick and easy access to such information—what policy
> makers sometimes refer to as transparency—the public can know
> what is expected of an owner and serve as supplemental "eyes and
> ears" to a more formal inspection protocol.[24]

The authors go on to argue that the key to members of the public developing an active proprietary interest is encouraging greater public use of a space. Referring to the ideas of William H. Whyte, the authors maintain that "use begets more use" and if a space is of "sufficient quality to make people want to use it in the first place . . . people will take a proprietary interest and help safeguard its continuing provision according to the applicable legal mandates." Further, the role of the city and interested private nonprofit groups is to "facilitate the use of public space, by describing them, as in this book, and by adopting a curatorial mentality." In order to increase public use, the authors encourage events such as "[r]oving art exhibits and traveling concert series." Such events would then "enable the public to conceive of these spaces as part of a larger system offering great value to the life of the City."[25] They presume that when the public develops this kind of proprietary interest they will be moved to check up on the provision of amenities and the opening hours listed on the plaques, and to report any discrepancies to the Department of City Planning. The authors conclude: "it is up to institutions of government, the private not-for-profit world, and the private sector as well as members of the public, to assure that this physical space is provided in its most alluring form."[26]

But how can the public feel proprietary about a space they do not collectively own and that is governed by processes to which they have little or no access? It is quite easy to see why the building owner's interests are significantly stronger than those of the public. To Minskoff, the atrium is part of his private property. Whether or not Minskoff is able to turn a profit depends on the perception of the building as formed in the minds of perspective clients. The appearance of the public space is directly related to the image of the building. One could argue that the presence of a rotating exhibit of works of art presents a more salable image than, for example, three stands of bamboo and a lot of loiterers. While it may seem a bit of a stretch to say that Minskoff's decision to exhibit art was mercenary because it would train members of the public to be art lovers and therefore bolster the price of his own collection, Minskoff did recognize that the presence of art enhances the perceived value of a building. The benefits to PaceWildenstein as the co-organizers of the exhibitions was also indirect but sizable. While it could not sell any of the artwork that was on display in the atrium, its corporate profile and the profile of its artists were raised through the exhibitions and exhibition press coverage.[27]

## After the Bamboo

The month before the atrium reopened, Minskoff violated the provisions of the special permit by closing the atrium from November 3 to 7, 1995. In a letter reminding Minskoff of his contractual obligations, Nicholas Fish, then chair of Community Board Five, added that "[s]ince Community Board Five strongly supported your application to modify the public space, I feel it is my duty now to express my grave concern."[28] Minsksoff claimed that the closures were necessary to the installation of the artwork. He also admitted that he held a private event in the space during this time. Unauthorized closures are nothing unusual in the scheme of the POPS program. What is unusual about the post-renovation conflict over the IBM Atrium is the level of disappointment expressed by those involved in the decision-making process. Even those people who had a voice in the negotiations over the space expressed disappointment in the process and its results. Minskoff not only violated opening hours, but also failed to comply with provisions for the management of the sculpture display.

For example, part of the agreement was that there would be an advisory committee that would "help to ensure the broadest possible participation of major 20th Century sculptors."[29] This was in part to prevent Minskoff and PaceWildenstein from exhibiting only the work of PaceWildenstein clients. The advisory board was described in a resolution dated March 9, 1995:

> An advisory council, with Community Board Five as a member, will be established to ensure both the broadest possible participation of major Twentieth Century sculptors in rotating exhibitions and the inclusion of artists represented by and in a diverse group of galleries and museums. This council is not intended to serve in either a controlling curatorial or bureaucratic manner.[30]

Between 1995 and 1999, the advisory board met only once, or at least Community Board Five was involved in only one meeting. In a 1996 memo, one member of the advisory committee who was also a member of Community Board Five stated that she felt "duped" by Minskoff and PaceWildenstein:

> I believe that it [the Sculpture Garden at 590 Madison Avenue] is both a disappointment and a sham. You cannot imagine how it saddens me to say this, as I feel so duped, and like I misled the Board. The biggest fear, addressed very clearly in the Board's resolution, was that the space would be perceived as a commercial extension of PaceWildenstein Galleries. Not only is this the perception, but it is, in fact, close to the truth.[31]

The writer pointed out that the only show to run between June 1996 and November 1996 was Alexander Calder, who is represented by PaceWildenstein. She also noted that the opening show was dominated by PaceWildenstein-represented artists, that a sign for the exhibition had PaceWildenstein's name on it, that PaceWildenstein had not returned calls regarding the scheduling of advisory committee meetings, that in 1996 the advisory committee had met only once, and, finally, that none of the outreach or educational programs discussed during advisory board meetings had been developed.

> Why I was foolish enough to believe that a real estate developer and a commercial gallery would act in a selfless, altruistic manner for the people of New York City is beyond me. . . . Unless we can change the current situation, I would recommend that we take action against any and all future approvals regarding PaceWildenstein, as represented by Marc Glimcher, and 590 Madison, as represented by Edward J. Minskoff.[32]

This letter indicates that many of the concerns raised in the review process regarding conflict of interest between the building owner and the management of the public space were well-founded. Minskoff did use the sculpture garden as an excuse to close the atrium to the public. Minskoff and PaceWildenstein did use the sculpture garden to promote artists that PaceWildenstein represented. Minskoff did disregard aspects of his contract, and responded only after repeated attempts at contact were followed by threats. Some concerns were raised by Community Board Five, others by the Municipal Art Society. These groups were part of the review process only because the Department of City Planning decided to invite them to review Minskoff's proposal. Because the planning department categorized the renovation of the atrium as a minor modification, they could have come to a decision with no input from outside reviewers. Only the City Planning Commission was required to be part of the review.

The problem with categorizing renovations as *major* or *minor* when there is no definition to work by is that the decision of what requires review and what doesn't can be arbitrarily assigned by the City Planning Commission on a case-by-case basis. All the control over what can and can't be changed in a POPS falls in their hands. They may, of course, decide to include some kind of review process, but they are not required to do so. What is most shocking about this lack of clear definition and the way this can be used to prevent public input is that it is anything but a bureaucratic oversight. While it is difficult to say that the law was originally intentionally vague so as to give this latitude to the City Planning Commission, it is possible to argue that the law is being kept vague for that reason.

Just two years prior to the controversy over the IBM Atrium, a similar controversy erupted across the street at the AT&T Building. In 1992 the Sony Corporation took over the former AT&T Building, and proposed to enclose what was an exterior space as an interior atrium. This change was even more drastic than the change at the IBM Atrium, and it was considered minor. Richard Schaffer, former chair of the City Planning Commission, received complaints about the commission's handling of the review process. Ruth Messinger, former president of the borough of Manhattan, argued that "the community should not have to depend on an applicant's goodwill to obtain meaningful input into a project modification." She stated, "the absence of clear criteria establishing thresholds for the distinction between major and minor modifications" is "unacceptable" because it "allows the City Planning Commission and the Department of City Planning to make

BAMBOOZLED?

arbitrary determinations which are likely to allow significant changes to escape appropriate public and administrative review."[33] Michael Presser, chairman of Community Board Five, raised the same concerns. Community Board Five unanimously passed a resolution in the summer of 1992 calling for the City Planning Commission to "act promptly to establish firm guidelines and thresholds for review of modifications to previously approved special permits in order to eliminate the appearance of arbitrariness and favoritism and to guarantee a fair review."[34]

In light of these serious concerns that were shared by the borough president, the chief elected official of the entire borough of Manhattan, and every member of Community Board Five, the response from Schaffer, the chair of the City Planning Commission, is astonishing. He simply explained the legal structure surrounding modifications to POPS as the structure stands. He states that modifications to POPS are subject to a Uniform Land Use Review Procedure "unless they require new waivers, authorizations or special permits under additional sections of the Zoning Resolution, or propose additional waivers or authorizations under the same sections but beyond the scope of those originally granted." He said that this legal structure works because it "allow(s) modifications to proceed by the most reasonable method possible, consistent with the nature of the changes requested." He argued that "imposing elaborate procedures" would in many cases be "wasteful of administrative resources." He further argued that the best approach is for the City Planning Commission and Department of City Planning to set up "additional procedures" on a case-by-case basis when proposed changes "involve more than routine details of design or function."[35]

The process Schaffer describes is exactly the process that both Community Board Five and the borough president criticized as being too open to arbitrary decisions. Schaffer did not address the concerns over or even acknowledge the possibility of such serious problems. Nor did he address the fact that changes might be made to a POPS that require no new special permit but that significantly change the quality of that space. Schaffer's description of public processes as "additional procedures" that may be "wasteful of administrative resources" indicates a belief that efficient bureaucracy is more important than opening the review process to broader scrutiny. His response also indicates a very particular stance to the legal foundations of the POPS program. He describes the law as it stands, and does not engage in a discussion of how it might be changed to reflect the real concerns of members of the public and their elected representatives.

The controversy over the atrium highlights specific issues around the "publicness" of New York's POPS not because of who is allowed to use them or for what purpose, but because of who is allowed to make decisions about how the spaces are changed over time. The POPS program itself must be changed to include not only public access to the physical spaces but also public access to the decision-making processes. Why does the Department of City Planning seem to see itself more as a mediator between "the public" and "the building owner" rather than as part of the public itself, advocating for public interests? This revision of the review process must also ask whether review by elected officials is even sufficient. David McGregor, architect and former director of planning for Manhattan for the New York City Planning Commission, argued that "[s]ince these are public spaces, the public ought to have a say about them. Then if we don't like what our elected and appointed public officials do, we can throw the bums out the next time."[36] But should waiting for the next election and casting a vote against someone you think made a bad decision be the level of possible public involvement in these processes? Or should the changes to the POPS program include bureaucratic processes for direct rather than representational involvement? And do the public officials who would be involved in making decisions about the space really represent the public of that space? Many people who use the atrium every day are office workers taking a break. They most likely live outside Manhattan. Others may be visiting New York from other states or countries. The POPS program went through a major rewriting process in 1975 in order to increase the requirements of building owners to provide more and better physical amenities in exchange for the financial incentives they receive. There is no reason why the program cannot be rewritten again to ensure that changes to the spaces are open to public and not quasi-public review.

However, even if this important link between POPS and the public spheres that govern them is mended, there are other fundamental problems with the program's policy and the specific spaces it has created that also prevent them from being dynamic public spaces. These problems arise because of the clash of values brought to these spaces by private developers, the planning department, and the people who claim them. The next two chapters examine spaces adjacent to IBM: Sony Plaza and Trump Tower. Whereas at IBM, changes in the plaza's design revealed underlying problems with the POPS decision-making processes—problems that preclude these spaces from having active public spheres—design at Sony and Trump acts upon the public itself.

# 5 Targeted Publics and Sony Plaza

Sony is about communication, dealing with people—
music, movies, video . . . they wanted to dispel the
elitist image and engage the building with the ground
and make it participatory.
   —*Charles Gwathmey, architect in charge of
   Sony Plaza design*

**Directly across the street** from the former IBM building is one of the most recognizable skyscrapers in Manhattan, the former headquarters of AT&T. The tower's stature (at 648 feet, more than 200 feet taller than IBM) and unique "broken pediment" style roof give it a distinctive and controversial presence. *New York Times* architectural critic Paul Goldberger called the building "one of the most startling skyscrapers of the last generation,"[1] while others commented that its roof was "more appropriate for a piece of furniture."[2] Love it or hate it, the tower remains unmistakable, even in mid-town's competitive skyline (Figure 5.1).

Built in 1984, Johnson's marble-clad tower presented an image of stability and solidness for AT&T in the years immediately following the now-infamous antitrust suit.[3] AT&T chose Johnson because he was the most recognized architect in America. Johnson achieved his iconic status in part because of the unique qualities of his buildings,[4] his reputation as a New York design powerbroker, and his own imitable look (versions of his perfectly round black spectacles are still donned by architecture students worldwide).[5] The importance to AT&T of a high-profile architect is highlighted by Johnson's comments on the way his firm was selected for the job.[6] He claims

Figure 5.1. Philip Johnson's AT&T Building with IBM on the left and Trump Tower on the right, 2001.

he did not even read the request for proposals that AT&T sent to his office: "[t]oo many irrelevant questions, I told them that when they called up. But we got the job anyway."[7]

The new AT&T headquarters rose stories above its neighbor, IBM. At the time, both AT&T and IBM produced computers, and both would soon be providing long-distance telephone services. An article in the *Economist* announcing the construction of the AT&T headquarters commented that "[s]tage sets are going up in midtown for America's biggest ever clash of corporate titans," adding that not only would AT&T be able to "look down on their rivals" but that they had hired the "more famous architect."[8] Johnson's signature did not come cheaply. As he himself admitted, the AT&T Building was about $20 million over budget.[9]

AT&T was able to create such a giant tower and reap the benefits of its prominence because of bonuses they received by providing two types of POPS: open-air pedestrian arcades on the northern and southern sides, and a covered pedestrian space running between the main building and a three-story annex (Figures 5.2 and 5.3). The covered pedestrian space was purportedly patterned after the Galleria in Milan. As in the IBM Atrium, the AT&T pedestrian space had movable tables and chairs, landscaping, and kiosks, but for the first time in the bonus program, the POPS at AT&T also included a science museum that was free and open to the public. The science museum, called AT&T Infoquest, was "dedicated to a multi-media presentation using the historic achievements in communications science and the latest technological advancement developed by Bell Laboratories as a core of the presentation."[10] The City Planning Commission considered the museum to be an important part of AT&T's special permit because the museum would increase pedestrian traffic and encourage use of the space.[11] A description of Infoquest in the New York *Blue Guide* from the museum's later years[12] said, this "hands-on museum of technology . . . should delight the technophile, young or old."[13] Infoquest had exhibitions on microchips, computers, and communications technology. Some exhibits were designed as games with which children could "direct their own rock video, manipulate a robot or program a computer to respond to voice commands."[14]

When AT&T reshuffled its office holdings in 1992, it leased the building to Sony. With Gwathmey Siegel & Associates Architects, Sony undertook a major redesign of the building's interior, including the open-air arcade, transforming the building to match Sony's carefully crafted corporate brand.[15] The transformation included a complete restructuring of the building's POPS. A 1993 *New York Times* article described the refurbishment of the AT&T Building and its transformation into a Sony icon: "Mr. Schulhof is redesigning the building's entire interior, with one goal in mind: Give the world at large a visible taste of what Sony's all about."[16] At the time, Microsoft, Nike, and Sony were leading the world in corporate branding, emphasizing marketing over production, image over object. As Naomi Klein has argued, branding requires an "endless parade of brand extensions, continued renewed imagery for marketing and, most of all, fresh new spaces to disseminate the brand's idea of itself."[17] With its combination of skyline presence, Madison

**95**

Figure 5.2. Original AT&T galleria, 1992. Courtesy of Dianne Harris.

Figure 5.3. Original AT&T arcade, 1992. Courtesy of Dianne Harris.

Avenue address, highly visible retail space, interior public space, and the Sony Wonder Technology Lab—Sony's version of Infoquest—Sony's new complex promised to be a potent brand booster.

The story of the transformation of the POPS and its ongoing programming and management offer points of entry into the complex and contradictory values that underlie Sony Plaza and the entire POPS program. Whereas the IBM controversy revealed that the program institutionally precluded active public spheres from developing around even well-designed and well-used spaces, the Sony controversy shows how the design, programming, and management of POPS can influence what people do there and even whether they are allowed to be physically present. If public spaces are to act as physical locations for participation in democratic activities—where people recognize themselves as part of publics in which they formulate positions about public life and/or in which they express these positions—all groups and individuals must have equal access. As Nancy Fraser has stated, in public spheres, who participates and on what terms matters.[18] The same is true of dynamic public spaces. At Sony Plaza, the terms on which one enters, occupies, and acts in the plaza are not equal, because to Sony, people are not equal. Sony welcomes some people as members of the Sony family, and rejects others who appear to be poor or homeless. The POPS program does little to counter the corporate sorting of public life.

## Public Space Calculus

In order to make changes to the existing AT&T bonus spaces, Sony had to clear their plans with the Department of City Planning and the City Planning Commission. Correspondence, testimony, and discussion from the City Planning Commission's public meeting reveal conflicting values toward public space: what should happen there, how it should relate to activities such as shopping and entertainment, and how corporate values relate to public values. Sony's proposal was controversial. It involved an overall loss of about 33 percent of publicly accessible square footage. The original 14,102 square feet of exterior open arcade was reduced to 3,542 square feet, because the rest was enclosed and converted to indoor retail space. The covered pedestrian space was increased from 5,625 square feet to 9,731 square feet (Figure 5.4).[19] Sony successfully argued that the original arcade space was inhospitable, windy, and cold and that the newly designed public areas, though significantly smaller, would have amenities that, according to planning

TARGETED PUBLICS AND SONY PLAZA

department incentive rules, would result in a similar net public benefit. They would be climate controlled and have seating areas and a public restroom.

Paul Goldberger praised the proposed arcade's new relationship to the street saying, "a solid facade with storefronts is better on Madison Avenue than the present open facade broken up by columns." He wrote positively about the plaza and its location within the building: "public space belongs off the Avenue, in the glass-roofed arcade, which even now is a far more successful space than the one in front." He also saw the overall reduction of publicly accessible space due to its transfer to private retail use as a fair trade:

Figure 5.4. Plan of Sony bonus spaces. Drafted by Vincent deBritto. Courtesy of New York Department of City Planning.

E 56th Street

SONY Wonderlab

restrooms

SONY Style

lobby

Starbuck's

Exhibit Area

Madison Avneue

E 55th Street

0          50

SONY Building

Privately owned public space in SONY Building—destination space

Privately owned public space in SONY Building—covered arcade

source: new york department of city planning

Somewhere there are people who like the A.T.&T. space as it is, but I doubt there are many. I would trade 18,947 feet of fair-to-middling space, which is what the building now has, for 10,220 feet of inviting and usable space any day. And if this important work of architecture ends up with an improved look in the bargain, so much the better.[20]

Not everyone shared Goldberger's assessment of the bargain. A letter to the editor of the *New York Times* written by Patricia McCobb of the League of Urban Landscape Architects stated that the new enclosed space would be "as private and controlled as a suburban mall."[21] At the public meeting held by the City Planning Commission in August 1992, additional concerns were raised. An attorney for the operator of a snack kiosk argued that the proposed changes should be put through a more stringent review process.[22] Harry Simmons Jr., who worked for Johnson and Burgee and had argued for the original special permits from the City Planning Commission, stated that the proposed changes would destroy the character of the building and that the interior spaces would be less accessible than the original exterior spaces. McCobb also testified that day. Her statement pointed to the tension between the legal language of the zoning code and how it represents and enforces a view of public space:

> Open space advocates of this city are troubled by the lack of debate over Sony's proposed filling in of almost 9,000 square feet of public open space. . . . What is even more alarming to us is that space given to the public in exchange for increased floor area is being removed from the public realm without discussion beyond convoluted zoning formulas which bring us to the startling conclusion that less does equal more.[23]

Charles Gwathmey, the architect hired by Sony to design the new arcade, argued that retail was part of a "tradition of strollers and people hanging around" and that "that kind of shopping, is very much about the public domain and about participation, and that's clear."[24] Philip Johnson, the AT&T Building's architect, argued in favor of the changes, saying the Sony proposal would increase retail along Madison Avenue and that the "shopping feeling" there was important to "respect[ing] the uses of the public."[25] Johnson even compared his arcade to the IBM Plaza across the street:

> our arcade . . . has proven to be a bit dark . . . I go across to my friendly competitor's, Mr. Barnes' building, the IBM, and I have a

**100**

friendly cup of coffee, in friendly surroundings in a friendly atmosphere, with friendly trees around me. I think that's one of the ideal public spaces around. The sign is too small, but it didn't keep me out and I'm a pretty trashy person.[26]

The sign Johnson referred to is the one announcing the fact that the IBM Atrium is open to the public. His contention that he felt free to walk in and enjoy a "friendly cup of coffee" even though he is a "pretty trashy person" was not only flippant, considering the number of New Yorkers who have experienced exclusion from spaces, but also oddly prophetic, given the events that would unfold in the redesigned Sony Plaza.

Even if members of the New York Planning Commission had their doubts as to whether the proposed Sony spaces would be of equal or greater public benefit when compared to the existing arcade and covered pedestrian space, they would have had little recourse to stop the changes. The zoning resolution that sets out the POPS program has strict calculations regarding the benefit of different kinds of spaces, and Sony had done its math. At the hearing, Michael Silverman, a representative for Sony, more or less "sealed the deal" by laying out the land-use calculations in order to argue that no special permit was needed for the changes. Silverman responded to planning commission concerns that the new spaces would not be as "public" by referring to the Zoning Resolution. He pointed out that "The Zoning Resolution . . . does not have a term called public space. It speaks of arcade; it speaks of plaza; it speaks of covered pedestrian space and other things."[27] His argument laid out the Sony proposal against the numeric formulas of the bonus program. He noted that the new Sony spaces, because of the amenities they would provide, would result in an even higher bonus than before.[28] He argued that the commission legally *had* to allow the changes. He also pointed out that the proposed spaces would nearly double the amount of climate-controlled pedestrian space, "which has been judged by you as legislators to have a great utility to the public by virtue of the fact that you give it a bonus rate that is almost four times higher than that for an arcade." He added that the proposed changes were not only developed within the confines of the bonus program, but also that the spaces were qualitatively better than Johnson's bonus spaces because they were "year-round spaces . . . more usable by the public."[29]

While Silverman didn't come out and say that the commission would open itself up to litigation if they tried to block the Sony project, his message was clear. Sony's plan met the requirements set out in the Zoning Resolution, and if the commission denied the request, they would have no legal language to justify their decision. Any arguments made regarding how "public" the new spaces would be had no legal traction because the resolution included no language about public space at all.

## Inside Sony Plaza

Today the Sony Plaza is considered one of the best POPS produced through the bonus program in part because of the number of its "public amenities."[30] Like the IBM Atrium, Sony Plaza is accessible from the street, its major spaces occur on one level, and it includes movable tables, chairs, and plantings. As at both Trump Tower and the IBM Atrium, you can get coffee and something quick to eat at Sony Plaza. As at Trump Tower, the public restroom and telephones at Sony Plaza are difficult to find but they exist. And because of the Sony Wonder Technology Lab, the plaza is often animated by the voices of groups of youngsters waiting in line.

As a result of the reconfiguration, Sony Plaza includes an intense mix of public space and commercial space in an interior setting. Sony Plaza is linked to a Sony store, where visitors can buy a piece of the Sony image at prices ranging from around $15 for a CD by a Sony-contracted artist to around $15,000 for a Sony home entertainment center. It is not simply that the public space exists next to the retail space; rather, in the case of Sony Plaza the public space is surrounded by private spaces. Because the plaza is nested within the building, the plaza's walls are also the exterior walls for Sony meeting rooms and the Sony Wonder Technology Lab.

The materials used in the design of Sony Plaza tie its image to that of Sony's corporate spaces. The plaza's walls are covered in the same pinkish-colored granite used for the building's exterior, but the walls on the western side are pierced by curved and rectangular glass bays, through which one can glimpse a hip-looking board room or the neon-lit entrance to Sony Wonder or a flat-screen video monitor announcing the presence of Sony Wonder. On the eastern side, the bottom half of the walls are clear windows to Starbucks and the Sony store, but the upper walls are covered with banners, some with abstract techno-style drawings and some simply stating "Sony." To the far northern end of the plaza is the Sony Wonder Technology Lab's exposed, bright yellow elevator. While there are no trees within the space, there are tall pyramidal topiaries of ivy. The furnishings in the space—tables, chairs, and trash receptacles—are all made of shiny aluminum. The message of the design is clear. The plaza is part of Sony. The cohesion of the aesthetic of metal, marble, and bold colors from the Sony palette pulls the space together in and of itself but also situates it within the aesthetic of the Sony brand.

Sony Plaza is perhaps most used and liveliest during the run-up to the December holidays. The giant topiary cones are covered in tiers of curling red and hot pink ribbons, their bases covered in upholstered red velvet fabric that complements the red "Sony" in the Sony Wonder sign. The floors are illuminated by hot pink, red, and yellow patterns of snowflakes projected from the ceiling trusses. A giant, white, translucent "tree" is banded with aluminum and framed by a red velvet curtain suspended from black steel trusses (exposed trusses in silver, black, and white factor large in the design of the plaza, the Sony store, Starbucks, and Sony Wonder, creating a minimalist-techno look). The cold weather brings people into the plaza that may otherwise have been outside. One Saturday morning there were five concurrent games of chess being played, with many onlookers. On such wintry days during the holiday season, it would seem that Johnson's description of the IBM Atrium as a place for a "friendly cup of coffee, in friendly surroundings in a friendly atmosphere, with friendly trees around me" could be used to describe Sony Plaza.

## "BB, Am I Pretty?" Public Museums and Target Markets

Perhaps the friendliest person at Sony Plaza is not a person at all but a robot named BB (Figure 5.5). Part mayor of the space and part entertainer, BB greets visitors from the plaza's south entrance and chats with them as they wait in line to enter Sony Wonder.[31] BB is portly and wears a loose-fitting (if you can call molded plastic "loose") white lab jacket over a blue button-down shirt with tie. He has a small antenna-like protrusion coming out of his bright yellow helmet/head. He sports a pocket protector with two bright, cartoonish pens. The cogs and wires that operate his eyes and jaw are visible. BB is able to turn his body and head to face whoever speaks to him, and is able to lower his eyes when he converses. BB looks like the perfect techno-sidekick: nonthreatening, a little goofy, and innocent. But BB is a carefully choreographed marketing machine, as is Sony Wonder.[32]

At Sony, debates over the new plaza's design included concerns that the space would become a physical advertisement for its corporate patron.[33] Sony's use of the plaza as a physical advertisement is much more nuanced and arguably more insidious than Donald Trump's use of Trump Tower. It

Figure 5.5. Girls talking to BB the Wonderbot, 2001. One asked, "BB, am I pretty?"

involves a carefully choreographed aesthetic experience, one based on classic design themes: inside and outside, and insider and outsider. As Naomi Klein has pointed out, branding involves a kind of seduction that takes place in "a venue that is part shopping center, part amusement park, part multimedia extravaganza—an advertisement more potent and evocative than a hundred billboards."[34] The goal of the branded environment is to go beyond advertising's goals of having people equate a product with a positive feeling to create instead a "lived reality."

The fact that a corporation as branding-savvy as Sony would develop and build a public space cum sales machine is hardly surprising. What is surprising is that the main marketing mechanism is an "amenity" required by Sony's contract with the city: Sony's version of AT&T Infoquest. Arguably Infoquest was also a kind of museum advertisement with exhibits that were set up to "delight the young technophile."[35] However, AT&T was not marketing to kids. For Sony, kids ages four to seventeen are a valuable market.

**104**

They also happen to be a segment of the public least able to distinguish a sales pitch from factual information. In the late 1980s, Sony began marketing My First Sony products to kids and found that the children's market was becoming one of the fastest growing in the electronics industry. In the early 1990s, around the same time that Sony was revamping the AT&T Building to better reflect its brand, Sony Music entered into a deal with Nickelodeon, then the largest producer in the world of children's television programming. Then-president of Sony Music in the United States, Thomas D. Mottola commented: "This agreement marks a significant step in Sony Music's expansion into the children's and family entertainment areas." Tom Freston, chair of MTV Networks[36] added, "Nickelodeon's knowledge of kids together with Sony Music's expertise in home video marketing and distribution is a powerful combination." Nickelodeon's senior vice president of consumer products described the network as "TV's all-purpose clubhouse for today's kids—a place they feel is their home base." He said that until the merger, kids never had "a comparable sense of ownership" in the home video market, adding, "[w]e're about to change that."[37]

As the sequel to AT&T's Infoquest, Sony Wonder is a required portion of its contract with the New York City Planning Department. But even if it is open to the public for free, Sony Wonder is also undeniably a marketing machine that draws thousands of visitors from Sony's key demographics— in particular, children ages four to seventeen. The Sony Wonder Technology Lab is a branding environment designed to initiate kids into the Sony community. On my first visit to Sony Plaza, I asked a Sony employee what Sony Wonder was all about. He replied, "It's a museum." "A museum of what," I asked? Without any hint of irony, he replied, "of Sony products." This is not how the museum is described either by Sony or by the New York City Planning Department, both of which refer to Sony Wonder as a "public museum of technology."

While children are transformed in Sony Plaza into Sony insiders, others are pushed out. As children line up to see the Sony spectacle, guards circle past the rows of tables and chairs ready to enforce the plaza's codes of conduct (Figure 5.6). These codes of conduct target people who are homeless by prohibiting otherwise legal behaviors. Attempts by homeless advocates to challenge Sony on their exclusive management practices reveal the inability of our legal system to protect those most reliant on our public spaces for their daily lives. Denying access to certain publics and transforming others into consumers threatens the relationship between physical public

spaces and active public forums. For homeless people, it becomes impossible to be present in the space at all, let alone to gather with peers in order to formulate positions regarding shared public lives. For children, it becomes impossible to recognize oneself and one's peers as part of a public and not simply as shoppers.

If there were ever a poster-boy/girl for the trade-offs involved in public-private partnerships for the provision of public spaces, BB would be it. BB and Sony believe it is in the interest of children to visit Sony Wonder. And Sony's target market, unlike AT&T's, and by far the largest portion of the summer "public" of this space, is children. What awaits children and adults who visit Sony Wonder is a model of brand seduction,[38] but the journey begins in Sony Plaza, where children interact with BB as they wait in line to enter. BB stands about five feet off the ground. As kids talk to him, they look up at his face. Even though BB's responses are fairly lackluster, it is oddly compelling to watch these interactions, mainly because of the children. I was amazed by the questions they asked BB. Some questions came up over and over again, such as "Are you a boy or a girl," to which BB replied by explaining that he/she was a robot, or pretended not to understand gender distinctions. Other questions were almost painfully sincere. One preteen girl asked, "BB, am I pretty?" "Yes, I think you are *all* pretty," BB replied diplomatically. A young boy asked, "BB, do you like me?" BB's answer to this one was, "But I don't know you." As BB answered, you could see the kids alternating between trying to figure out how he worked and energetically testing him with questions. One child asked, "Are you human?" BB replied, "What is a human?"

The riddling and watching continues until groups are called into the entrance, where, at the time of one visit, a sign read: "Have a Sony Wonderful Holiday!" Once inside, you visit the counter, give your zip code, and receive a swipe card. You see a set of video displays behind the ticket counter that shows what BB sees through his video-camera eyes. Next, visitors ride in the

Figure 5.6. The plaza's codes of conduct are printed on small menu-like cards and placed on the tables. They state: "To ensure the public's use and enjoyment of SONY Plaza, the following are prohibited: sleeping, loitering, or disorderly conduct; smoking or drinking alcoholic beverages; shopping carts, obstructions, or unattended packages; gambling or promoting gaming; crowding or blocking doorways or walkways; playing of loud music, radios, or stereos; obscene language or gestures; running, skating, or bicycling; bringing in pets or animals other than animals assisting the physically challenged; creating any conditions that unreasonably pose a health or safety risk or disturb others."

clear cylindrical elevator, from which they can look down on the plaza and the crowd around BB. The elevator doors open into a dark space lit only by thousands of small star-like bulbs built into a black wall. The group is escorted into another starlit room where they all "personalize" their swipe card. A friendly face on a video screen (the screen can be raised or lowered to the eye level of the visitor) instructs you to record a voice sample and your picture (Figure 5.7). The individual log-in kiosks are made of brushed stainless steel.

Before you can move between various spaces in the museum, you must run your swipe card through readers that are positioned at each threshold. As a result, Sony can record how long you lingered in each section and the exhibit can respond to your presence in each section. Your face appears on video screens next to footage of Jimmy Carter at Camp David (a la *Forrest Gump*), and your voice is heard in a display about music recording. Visitors are thus inserted into the Sony experience, becoming part of the organization, entwined in its history and world history at the same time. The sequence is organized chronologically, starting with and moving along through the videocassette recorder, the personal computer, and the compact disc player. All examples depicting the evolution of technology bear the Sony logo. The educational content of the displays is almost nonexistent. The stage labeled "radio" has only a sign that says "radio" and an example of an old radio and sounds that might be coming from it. The lesson is that the history of Sony is the history of technology.[39]

The highlight of this part of the exhibit, aside from seeing yourself on-screen, is seeing how BB works. It is as if the "man behind the curtain" has been revealed. BB is controlled by a Sony employee who watches and listens to plaza visitors who are talking to BB. The employee answers their questions and moves BB to make "eye contact." A sheet on the employee's workstation has a list of appropriate songs and possible answers to questions. Museum visitors can watch people in the plaza interact with the robot— people who, because they have not had the entire Sony Wonder experience, are still "out of the loop," not privy to Sony insider knowledge. It was just after passing by the BB control station and going down a ramp that included a multitude of screens showing clips of a young Frank Sinatra,[40] JFK, and the original "Sony Boy" that a door, not previously visible because it was a black door flush against a black wall, opened. A smiling young Sony employee stepped right in front of me. One of the museum employees

Figure 5.7. Child making an ID card at the Sony Wonder Technology Lab, 2002.

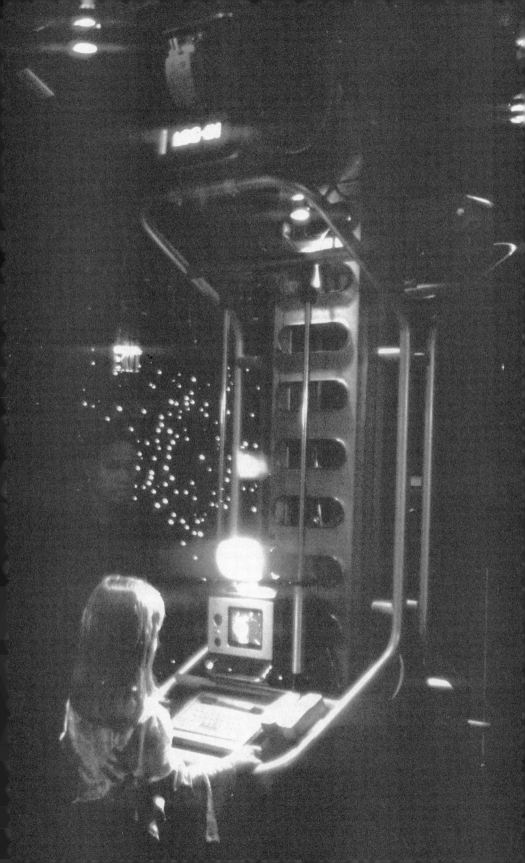

had noticed that I was taking a lot of pictures and she wondered why. Was I from the press? Did I know that I could not publish pictures from Sony Wonder for profit? I explained that I taught design and was photographing the space for class. Where did I teach? Did I have a business card? After several questions, I broke free from the conversation and continued through the museum.

From the museum of technology, you move down a series of ramps to either a high-definition movie[41] or into an area of technology learning where you can "learn" about TV production and ultrasound technology. This segment is followed by places where you can (finally) play the latest Sony PlayStation games. On the way out, you scan your card one final time and get your certificate of achievement. You reemerge where you began, and see another group of people enchanted by the mystery of BB. But now you know his secret. Before the glow of the Sony experience has worn off, you can enter a set of doors just on the other side of BB that lead into the Sony store, purchase a videogame or a CD by a Sony recording artist, get a cup of coffee at the attached Starbucks, and relax at one of the tables in the plaza without ever stepping outside or leaving Sony's embrace.

The Sony space embodies the trade-offs of linking commercial spaces and public spaces, particularly because children are involved and because of the sophistication of the Sony sales machine. A recent article published in *Nation* explores the importance of children—or, more specifically, the more than $28 billion of their own money and the $600 billion of their parents' money—to advertisers.[42] In order to successfully market to kids, advertisers are turning to psychologists: almost every kid-focused advertising team has at least one psychologist. That companies use child psychologists to develop more sophisticated marketing campaigns for kids is not all that shocking; it points to the importance of kids as a market. In 1999 the amount of money spent on advertising and marketing to kids reached $12 billion, "leaving kids bombarded with more than 40,000 manipulative ads a year on TV alone."[43] The *Nation* article goes on to discuss the cognitive abilities of children and children's inability to understand "persuasive intent." Sony Wonder is a valuable space of brand dissemination (Figure 5.8).

While children are courted at Sony Plaza, there are other members of the public that Sony would rather never visit: those who cannot purchase music, movies, or video. On top of every table in the plaza are little placards that look almost like menus but are instead codes of conduct.

Figure 5.8. Child looking at the merchandise in the Sony store window, 2002.

TARGETED PUBLICS AND SONY PLAZA

Sony (and several other interior-space managers) has been illegally enforcing codes of conduct in the plaza and has been discriminating against and allegedly mistreating homeless persons. The codes read: "To ensure the public's use and enjoyment of Sony Plaza, the following are prohibited: Sleeping, loitering or disorderly conduct, Smoking or drinking alcoholic beverages, Shopping carts, obstructions or unattended packages, Gambling or promoting gaming, Crowding or blocking doorways or walkways, Playing of loud music, radios or stereos, Obscene language or gestures, Running, skating or bicycling, Bringing in pets or animals other than animals assisting the physically challenged, Creating any conditions that unreasonably pose a health or safety risk or disturb others."

Two lawyers, Thomas Martin and Normal Siegel, worked with advocate Mark Luehrs to develop a case against Sony because of its plaza management practices. They alleged that Sony has been discriminating against plaza visitors who appear to be poor or homeless. Specific allegations included: guards recording the movements only of homeless people, guards bumping or shaking people awake who are sitting at tables, homeless people being asked to leave the space after two hours, and homeless people being denied access to the restrooms. They also argued that the codes of conduct that Sony vetted with the planning department and has posted on every plaza table are "so vague as to render it impossible to assure one's compliance—or to accurate and balanced enforcement."[44] Sony denied all allegations.

Whether Sony has made attempts to enforce their codes of conduct, the codes themselves parallel the National Law Center on Homelessness and Poverty (NLCHP) definition of criminalization of homelessness:

> practices of local jurisdictions in legislating against basic
> life-sustaining activities such as sleeping, sitting, or storing
> personal belongings in places where people are forced to
> exist without shelter. In addition, "criminalization" can
> include the selective enforcement of other laws like loitering
> or public intoxication against people who appear to be
> experiencing homelessness.[45]

The criminalization of homeless people is not something unique to Sony Plaza but is pervasive both in privately owned and publicly owned spaces in Manhattan, particularly in interior spaces with climate control. It is not within the scope of this chapter to discuss the overwhelming range of issues facing people who have no access to the private realm.[46] Nor has enough research been done on the specifics of Sony's antihomeless management techniques. But the degree of screening embedded in the design of Sony Plaza and the way its codes of conduct target the homeless make further study of this issue necessary.

Attempts at litigating for access to public space highlight the fact that legal aspects of public space are complex. There is not legal right to be in public space. In fact there is no *legal* definition of public space at all. Rather, the concept of the public forum, as it relates to civil liberties such as free speech, and state transportation laws regarding the management of public thoroughfares form the basis for much of the litigation surrounding the use of public space in New York City.

Lawyers like Martin and Siegel face several problems with legally challenging codes of conduct. First, until the codes are enforced—that is, until someone is forcibly removed from the space—there is no dispute. Without a dispute, there is no ruling. But to say that access is not limited without enforcement is incorrect. Sony and the Department of City Planning are using our culture's everyday conception of how the law is enforced to enforce standards of conduct. Second, developing cases is time-consuming. Because plaintiffs are homeless, it is difficult to maintain contact, particularly since some cases can take several years to develop and move through the courts. Even collecting statements is difficult. As is often the case in challenges to the neoliberal city, treating the effects does little to treat the causes:

> While this litigation has led to important victories and captured the public's attention (though not always its wholehearted support), it remains only a part of the picture. Suing over the right to emergency shelter or the right to panhandle on streets or sleep in parks is critical to many homeless people, but it does not address the underlying causes of homelessness, such as the crisis of affordable housing, decreasing income and public benefit levels, and lack of access to other needed services.[47]

If the 1975 and 1999 changes to the bonus program have led to a stringent accounting of physical elements in the spaces down to the number of trash receptacles, they did not raise the issue of ongoing problems of ensuring public access in privately owned public spaces. While each bonus space is required to list on a sign in the public space the amenities it must provide according to its contract, the Zoning Resolution says nothing regarding the owner's ability to manage public use of the space.

City Planning has taken the position that an owner may prescribe "reasonable" rules of conduct. In determining the definition of reasonable, the Department has looked at the rules of conduct applicable in City-owned parks for general guidance. Thus, for example, the Department has considered a dog leash requirement, a ban on the consumption of alcoholic beverages, or a prohibition on sleeping in an indoor space to be reasonable. . . . On the other hand, suggestions by owners that they be allowed to exclude "undesirable" persons on some basis other than improper conduct, or to set limits on the amount of time a member of the public may sit in or otherwise use a space, have been considered unreasonable.[48]

Who determines the rules for conduct in public spaces? Is it strictly up to the owner to set them according to its own preferences as a property owner, or does the Zoning Resolution's definition of a residential plaza as an open area for "public use" carry with it some notion of public rights as well? Under either view, reasonable rules and reasonable conduct are the touchstones.[49]

"Reasonable" to Sony and the New York City Planning Department includes rules that would, if enforced, be illegal. Put differently, anything that constitutes legal behavior outside Sony Plaza is also legal behavior within Sony Plaza. Sony does not "grant" access. All the rights and privileges due to individuals in public spaces must also be guaranteed in privately owned public spaces.[50] Any codes of conduct developed by private owners, sit upon the rights one has outside of the space. They are "brought in" as it were. But as the Sony case shows, litigating against codes of conduct is difficult and costly.[51]

## Conclusions

The actual "value"—that is, in dollars and cents—of interior public spaces can be found in the negotiations around bonus spaces between the Department of City Planning and the owners of POPS. Certain kinds of public spaces are simply worth more than others. Amenities considered more valuable yield more in the exchange. Sony's ability to convert larger portions of a formerly public space into private retail space hinged on the fact that square foot for square foot a smaller climate-controlled space yielded the same bonus allowance as a large space that was open to the elements. Sony was able to completely transform the former AT&T space in ways that allowed Sony to develop its brand, because in the "accounting" process of the POPS program an enclosed space was "worth more" to the public. As Sony's lawyer pointed out during the Planning Commission meeting, whether the new Sony Plaza would be "less public" as some on the commission charged didn't matter, because the contracts dealt with calculations and their numbers added up. Sony did agree to leave out the giant television screen and toned down some of the advertising, but whether they could convert the open-air arcade into a Sony store was a moot question.

The accounting process that weighs the value of amenities in POPS serves an important function. It gives the Department of City Planning the ability to weigh against the bonus it will receive, the investment that the corporation is making in the development and management of a POPS space. What the Sony case shows, however, is that the public is not a monolithic entity with uniform needs and desires. Therefore, public amenities are not equally necessary or desirable. On an individual basis, a warm place to sit for an hour for someone without a home is worth much more than it is to someone taking a break from the office or from shopping. Furthermore, to a corporation such as Sony, the public is not uniform. Arguably, during the holiday shopping season it is in the best interest of Sony to remove from the space people who look as if they are homeless, in order to make sure that potential shoppers feel as comfortable as possible. Perhaps the biggest problem is not in the actual accounting of the POPS program but the very idea that a single corporation with a billion-dollar name to protect could ever be the provider and manager of a physical public space when its members, in the corporation's eyes, are anything but equal.

Of course, homeless people face issues of criminalization and inequity whether they are in a privately owned public space or a publicly owned public space. What the Sony case reminds us of is that, as a country, we are a long way from the socioeconomic parity necessary for functioning public spheres. The distance between Sony's branding ideal as fed to kids at the Wonder Lab and the actual lives of many New Yorkers who are poor or homeless marks a divide in American society that underlies not only public spaces but also democracy itself. At a time when nonprofit programs that aid the homeless are under threat of having their federal funding cut if they also have programs that help homeless people register to vote, the links between public spheres and public spaces and the rights to be in a space and to participate in democratic life become all the more apparent, and the importance

TARGETED PUBLICS AND SONY PLAZA

of public spheres in advocating for rights to housing and to public space become all the more crucial.

What if the POPS program's accounting system was changed to reflect a different set of public "needs"? What if New Yorkers decided that providing shelter to those without access to private space was more important than a place for people to drink coffee and enjoy a break from shopping? Would Sony, in return for bonus incentives, transform the plaza into a shelter? What if Sony simply bought out of the program and that buy-out money was directed toward social programs that sought to bridge the gap between rich and poor? Does New York need another "friendly place to have a friendly cup of coffee"? These questions are, of course, for New Yorkers to decide, not Sony.

# 6 Trump Tower and the Aesthetics of Largesse

This luxury high rise is not only a place where the very rich live, but also where they shop. . . . It seems silly to call a place so decadent a mall.
—Shopping Guide, *www.ny.com*

This is not your low-income housing project . . .
of which we need many. But we also need
accommodations, uh, for those who can afford to pay
a lot of money and bring a lot of taxes into the city. . . .
You know there's nothing wrong with being rich . . .
the fact is . . . it's better to be rich, if you have a
choice, than to be poor.
—Ed Koch, *former New York City mayor, at the
building dedication for Trump Tower*

**The reality TV show** *The Apprentice* brought Donald Trump, and his hair, back into the American spotlight. During its first season in 2004 it was rated number one of new programs, with an average of 20.7 million viewers a week. The show's format is simple: a group of aspirant moguls is divided into teams. Each team performs the same business assignment, such as selling lemonade on the streets of New York or dreaming up an ad campaign for a luxury airline. At the end of the day everyone returns to Trump Tower, where Trump and two of his corporate henchmen scrutinize the aspirants' business acumen. After laying blame, arguing, and backstabbing, Trump makes the final cut, proclaiming, "You're fired!"

As *The Apprentice* has reacquainted the American viewer with Donald Trump, it has also, for the first time, acquainted many people with Trump Tower, the show's setting. The director uses the building to great dramatic effect. Verticality symbolizes power. The contestants' movements within Trump Tower correspond to their standing as competitors. While the aspirants live in "the Suite . . . a hip Manhattan loft apartment,"[1] Trump occupies the penthouse, several floors above. In an early episode, Trump rewarded that week's winning group of wannabes with a tour of his pad, which he described as "the best apartment in New York," adding that the only people who see it are usually "Presidents, kings."[2] The aspirants' temporary rise to the top is poignant because we know that at that very moment the others, the losers, are locked in life and death negotiations on a lower floor. One of them has to leave, and will leave later that night. The descent in rank of the week's loser parallels their descent through the building, across the lobby, over the sidewalk, and into a waiting cab. Or as Trump puts it, "from the suite to the street." From the cab, the loser may catch one last glimpse of Trump's glimmering tower, a jewel in Trump's ever-increasing personal fortune, a fortune that the week's loser will never be so close to again because of his or her shortcomings.

As a result of the show's success, people flock to Trump Tower to have their picture taken under a huge promotional sign that says "You're Fired!" But even before *The Apprentice* craze, Trump Tower and its shopping atrium were popular tourist destinations. The spaces are busiest on summer weekends, when tourist traffic includes groups visiting from cruise ships docked at the New York City Passenger Ship Terminal,[3] and during the holiday shopping season. Trump Tower's popularity is due not only to Trump's reputation but also to the building's dramatic interior—in particular, its seven-story pink marble waterfall. While many tourists visit Trump Tower, few may know that the waterfall graces what is legally a POPS, not just a glitzy shopping mall. Actually, the waterfall's atrium is part of a *system* of POPS in the tower, developed according to New York's Bonus Zoning Ordinance.

Like its neighbors in the Sony Building and at 590 Madison Avenue, the POPS of Trump Tower are nested within the building itself and include more than one type of bonus space. However, the Trump POPS system and its economic underpinnings are far more complicated than those of neighboring buildings. Trump Tower's POPS include the atrium, a passageway that connects the atrium to the POPS atrium at 590 Madison Avenue; a seating area, bathrooms, and telephones on the lower level; and two landscaped terraces on the fourth and fifth floors (Figure 6.1). As with adjacent properties, the Department of City Planning classifies the Trump Tower POPS as "destination spaces," or ones that draw visitors who live and work in the area as well as those from further afield.[4] In return for building and maintaining the POPS, Trump was able to build the tower much higher and therefore more profitably.

Even visitors who notice the "Open to the Public" signs[5] may not understand that Trump Tower is a masterpiece of real estate finance involving

TRUMP TOWER

millions of dollars in public incentives. The bonuses from the POPS program were only one part of an incredibly lucrative puzzle that included bonuses for all the building's retail square footage, transfer of air rights from a neighboring building, and generous city tax abatements for new housing.[6] Beneath all the glitter and glass lies a suite of zoning bonuses that Trump parlayed into one of the most profitable real estate projects ever built in New York City.

Like the economic structures behind most works of architecture, the underlying economics of Trump Tower are invisible to those who visit the building or who see it on TV. While we cannot see the economic foundations of the building, Trump Tower's

Figure 6.1. Bonus spaces in Trump Tower. Drafted by Vincent deBritto. Courtesy of New York Department of City Planning.

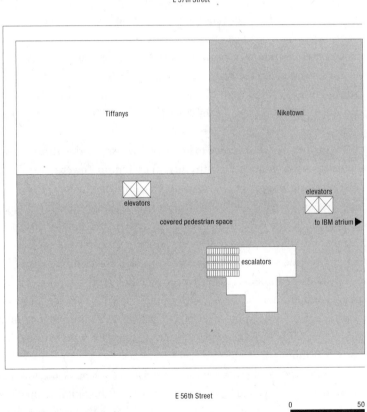

E 57th Street

Tiffanys

Niketown

Fifth Avneue

elevators

elevators

covered pedestrian space

to IBM atrium ▶

escalators

E 56th Street

0 _____ 50

Trump Tower

Privately owned public space on ground floor of Trump Tower

design, created by Der Scutt while he was partner in charge of design at Swanke Hayden Connell Architects,[7] does convey a message. The aesthetics of the POPS of Trump Tower—that is, the way the tower is experienced by the people who visit it—are potent and work in much the same way that the tower serves as the setting of *The Apprentice*. But rather than transforming Ivy League business students into Trump's novitiates, the aesthetic experience of moving through these POPS transforms the occupants of a public realm into visitors who have been temporarily and conditionally invited into Trump's private realm. The building's design "tells" us that Trump is much richer than any of us will ever be. What it doesn't tell us is that Trump's fortune is founded on public money.

For a design that is so potent, Trump Tower has received little critical attention from design writers, particularly in comparison to the amount of ink spilled over its neighbor, the AT&T Building. One possible and plausible reason (and one that was anonymously affirmed by a former architectural editor) is that Trump Tower was considered to be too tasteless for the architectural press to honor in print. A 1993 *Newsday* article that surveyed New York architects about their favorite indoor spaces found that most concurred: Trump Tower's spaces were "a spectacular ode to tackiness."[8] One architect who was interviewed said, "I think it's pretty horrible," but added, "It's very glitzy and people either love it or hate it."[9]

One person who seemed to love it, at least its interior atrium, was Paul Goldberger, who argued that "the atrium of Trump Tower may well be the most pleasant interior public space to be completed in New York in some years."[10] Goldberger called it "warm, luxurious and even exhilarating." He credited the design success of the atrium to the richness of the materials and the care with which it was crafted—in particular the Breccia Perniche marble that covered the walls and floors, which he said "gives off a glow of happy, if self-satisfied, affluence." Goldberger was, however, critical of the overall spatial configuration of the network of interior public spaces, in particular the long hallway that connected the waterfall-graced atrium to the building's entrance at Fifth Avenue, which he saw as too narrow to provide enough room for "milling or casual strolling."[11]

Goldberger was most critical of the faceted shape of the tower itself, noting that the "zigs and zags" of the exterior of the building provided increased views for each of the apartments, but that the tower's irregular form looked "hyperactive," particularly in comparison with its "serene" next door neighbor, Tiffany's.

**120**

In a sense, this sums up the essential design philosophy at work—in the process of achieving a balance between a building's public presence and its private one, the decision was made to make the private presence paramount . . . we have an exterior shape that succeeds in serving apartment dwellers first, and the relationship to neighboring buildings on the skyline and the street second.[12]

What is interesting about Goldberger's analysis is the way in which he assesses the building's relationship to the public good. He argues that the private condo owners are rewarded with more windows and better views because of the shape of the tower, but that its unusual shape in the context of its Fifth Avenue location gives the tower a "poor public presence." While a new skyscraper's shape may indeed visually detract from a city's skyline (whether or not this is the case at Trump Tower is open to debate), there is much more room for an examination of the building's role in New York's public life and the way its design exploits and masks the relationships between public and private money. Goldberger, albeit superficially, did raise an important issue: that the design of Trump Tower embodies tensions between public and private values. Goldberger focused on the conflict he saw between the shape of the tower that was designed to provide more windows for those inside the building versus those on the outside, who were forced to look at a structure that was unappealing.

But the relationships between design, the public good, and private gain at Trump Tower are more complex and significant to the relationships between public spaces and public spheres than whether a building's tower has a visually "poor public presence." The design of Trump Tower masks important information—precluding its ability to be a site and subject of active public spheres. In this chapter we will move through the spaces of Trump Tower and explore the connections between the building's design—including its spatial configuration, its materials, and detailing—the building's economic underpinnings, and the aesthetic experience the design creates.

The configuration of the spaces enabled Trump to procure massive public financing. The design masks the public qualities of the building's financing and reinforces Trump Tower as a symbol of Trump's private wealth. The public spaces are so enmeshed within the building that they are nearly impossible to understand as *distinguished from* the remainder of the tower or, for that matter, from the image of Trump and his corporation. Because of the physical arrangement of the spaces, the materials, the detailing, and the programming, members of potential publics who enter Trump

Tower view themselves and others as individuals enjoying the temporary hospitality of Donald Trump and are unable to recognize themselves as members of publics in a public space—a space whose very existence raises questions about what is good and right related to the public underwriting of private building projects.

## The Aesthetic Experience of Trump Tower

The aesthetic experience of Trump Tower—and the framing of the public as temporary visitors—begins even before one enters the building, perhaps even before one sees the building. The tower sits at the most expensive intersection of the most expensive shopping districts in Manhattan. A Trump-produced brochure aimed at potential condo buyers describes the mystique of the address:

> Fifth Avenue . . . Fifth Avenue across from the Plaza and Bergdorf Goodman. Fifth Avenue right next door to Tiffany's and Bonwitt Teller. Fifth Avenue with a sweeping view of New York City. St. Patrick's. Rockefeller Center. The Museum of Modern Art . . . the very hub of the international scene.[13]

New York City guidebooks and Trump's brochure are not the only places where one will find descriptions of Fifth Avenue as the elite shopping street of Manhattan. The city designated Fifth Avenue as a subdistrict of the Special Midtown District[14] and has written special building requirements for new construction and renovations that aim to "preserve . . . and enhance the character of the Fifth Avenue Subdistrict as the showcase of New York and national retail shopping . . . and tourist destination."[15] The special requirements include standards for sidewalk width, setbacks, the size and look of signage, and the kinds of things that can and can't be sold in the stores. As the *NYC Zoning Handbook*[16] states, special districts and their attendant incentive systems are ways to "use private capital to carry out public policy." In the case of the Fifth Avenue subdistrict, the public policy aims to maintain the street's elite status.

Because of Trump Tower's position within a district imbued with connotations of wealth, luxury, and economic exclusivity, our aesthetic experience of the Trump Tower public spaces are shaped even before we approach the POPS. Most visitors are already outsiders on Fifth Avenue. Its geographic location in the city delineates who will go there: those who work in the area, those who live there, or those who are sightseeing or shopping there. Shopping in the Fifth Avenue subdistrict is out of the reach of most New Yorkers. Most people who visit Trump Tower are window-shoppers and tourists.

Those who do find themselves in the neighborhood and who approach Trump Tower will find the entrance is set back from the sidewalk by about fifteen feet within a gleaming alcove of glass and brass. At the bottom of a sign that reads "Welcome to the World's Most Extraordinary Shopping Experience, TRUMP TOWER" and in letters half the size is printed "Atrium Open to the Public 8:00 AM to 10:00 PM." Rows of little gold Ts form a band across the smudge-free glass. Trump Tower may be the only POPS with its own doorman. Visitors may find the presence of a doorman a bit over the top, but the doorman at Trump Tower serves two functions. His presence marks the transition from public sidewalk to Trump Tower, or Trump's Tower. The implication is that if one is welcomed into a space, one can also be unwelcomed. The Trump doorman also acts as a screener, in contact with the security guards inside. These days the doorman is asked for his picture even more often than before, since people recognize him from *The Apprentice* (Figure 6.2). Perhaps his new status as a familiar TV figure will lessen his potential as a screener, since for some reason he now may seem more approachable, but the message remains "Welcome to Trump Tower." There is a good reason he is dressed as an old-time doorman, one who might work at a fancy hotel or an apartment building. While he welcomes visitors to a private realm, he also welcomes them to a private realm with a public image. He is equal part gatekeeper, greeter, and advertisement for the Trump way of living.

Of course, there are more direct ways of keeping people out of a POPS than posting a costumed doorman at the entrance, and Trump has tried those ways too. The planning department file on Trump Tower is packed with memos regarding Trump's noncompliance with his contracts. The complaints started in 1983, the same year Trump Tower opened. Trump closed the space for private parties and did not respond to requests from the Department of City Planning and others that he observe the legally required opening hours.[17] The tone of the memos becomes increasingly frustrated as Trump's infractions stack up. One internal memo suggested that a letter be written to Trump and his attorney to "inform them that the hours are 8 a.m. to 10 p.m., *every* day—including religious holidays and secular holidays even including leap year days."[18] One particularly frustrated citizen sent copies of

the letter to Mayor Ed Koch, adding a handwritten note at the bottom stating: "Obviously Mr. T cannot keep to even simple plans and restrictions. Please consider this in the future."[19] A staff member of the planning department described being asked to leave the tower. When she returned an hour or two later, the space was full of "very well dressed" partygoers. One internal memo dated July 10, 1985, told of security guards turning people away on a Saturday. The memo closed with "[o]ur perennial source of problems has sprung another."[20] I'm sure it wasn't very funny at the time, but looking back, the stack of memos, the increasingly frustrated tone of the whistleblowers, and Trump's seeming insistence on disregarding the contract seems so perfectly, well, Trump.

The city's early responses to Trump's repeated failure to meet the standards of his contract had little effect. Trump was forced to add more signage indicating the required opening hours and to announce that the spaces were open to the public, but Trump's noncompliance continued. The Department of City Planning threatened him with lawsuits and fines, but there is no record of actual fines being levied. Because of Trump's infractions, the planning department informed Trump they would be reviewing the entire area to make sure all the spaces in the building were in compliance with the conditions of the permit.[21]

As if to counter the Department of City Planning's complaints against him that year, Trump sent a handwritten memo to Philip Schneider of the Department of City Planning that read, "Phil—I thought you would enjoy reading the enclosed. It is one of many. Best, Donald." Attached to the memo was a letter dated December 15, 1984, two months after Trump closed the atrium, without city permission, for a private party.[22] The writer, a woman from Jackson Heights in Queens, said that she had visited Trump Tower with a friend the previous week and that she wrote because she "had to let them know about the sheer joy, pleasure and delight" they experienced. She added that they "were so deeply touched by the beauty of it all that neither one of us slept that night and we are still talking about it," and that she "could go on forever but will not because I'll run away with myself emotionally." She closed her note by saying, "Thank you, thank you, thank you for giving two middle class folks a glimpse into wonderland. God bless!!"[23]

If this note captures the aesthetic experience of Trump Tower as a place of luxury and spectacle, it also reveals how tied this aesthetic is to sensations of privacy and hospitality. The response of the visitor is one

Figure 6.2. Entrance to Trump Tower POPS with doorman, 2002.

of gratefulness to a private owner for the gift of that experience. Mrs. Lang-hammer and her friend were lucky that they hadn't visited on October 17, 1984, when Susan Leven took a seat by the base of the waterfall and was almost immediately told to leave the building. When Leven, a Department of City Planning employee, asked if the doorman knew that the space was public, he replied, "I'm asking you nicely."[24]

Langhammer's thank-you note confirms the overwhelming splendor of the Trump Tower aesthetic. Once inside, the reflectivity of the brass and polished marble is dazzling. One enters a long, wide hallway that slopes down into the building. It is not a place for milling around, and there is nowhere to sit. Instead, everyone walks forward toward the enormous marble waterfall. There are no fingerprints on the brass. There is no dust. Along the left-hand wall, perfectly groomed ficus trees emerge from a floor clean enough to eat off. On either side, display cases feature products from the Trump Tower shops, such as $500 gold-tipped fountain pens. The top of each display case is crowned with a thick brass T. During the holidays, the hallway is packed with tourists and the waterfall becomes a backdrop for a gigantic Christmas tree sparkling with lights. The tourists move forward slowly, mouths open, cameras ready for the shot (Figure 6.3).

While visitors entering the hallway are transformed into gaping-mouthed spectators, the hallway as a physical structure conducts its own economic metamorphosis. By linking the retail spaces that ring all levels of the atrium (Figure 6.4) to the protected Fifth Avenue subdistrict outside, the hallway transforms all of Trump Tower's retail square footage into space for which he received a zoning bonus. This bonus was perhaps Trump's biggest trump. As "The Donald" himself said, "I didn't need the rent from the (retail spaces of the) Atrium to make the project pay off . . . I only put the stores in because of the bonus."[25] The total bonus from the POPS and the retail amounted to an extra eight stories of tower. Trump said that at first he thought of just having three levels of retail inside, but changed his mind when he realized how many more apartments he could build if the retail went five floors up instead.

The Trump condominiums offer sweeping views of the city and Central Park—arguably one of the most coveted and costly views in Manhattan—because of another of Trump's zoning maneuvers. By buying the air rights over Tiffany's, his neighbor to the north, for $5 million, Trump prevented Tiffany's or subsequent building owners from increasing the height of

Figure 6.3. Hallway in Trump Tower during the holidays, 2003.

TRUMP TOWER

the building. In this way Trump was able to promise potential condo buyers protected views of Central Park *and* build his tower higher.[26] All the condos sold within three years, for a sum totaling $277 million—$87 million more than it cost to construct the entire building—including nineteen floors of office and retail.[27] Trump still owns the office and retail spaces and rents them out at some of the highest rates in Manhattan.[28]

Because most people who visit the building are drawn back toward the waterfall, they may not even notice the gleaming bank of elevators to the left (Figure 6.5). If they do, they might imagine—given the security check, the plainclothes guards, and the lack of clear signage—that these elevators lead to the private apartments and offices of the building. However, this is not the case. These elevators lead to more levels of shopping and to additional public spaces on upper levels of the building. But unlike the doorman at the front who welcomes most but certainly not all visitors to the building, the plainclothes guards do nothing to point out the well-appointed and much less crowded public spaces on the upper floors (Figure 6.6). Even if you are allowed to use the elevator, you must know what to ask for. You can't use the elevators by yourself, and must ask someone to take you to your destination. These floors are also accessible from the escalators near the waterfall, but again if you don't know what you are looking for, the upper POPS are difficult to find.

Figure 6.4. (*left*) Atrium escalators during the holidays, 2003.
Figure 6.5. (*below*) Elevators that lead to additional POPS, 2001.

Directly facing the elevators is another overlooked but very important part of the POPS of Trump Tower: a marble bench that is the only place to sit on the entire ground-floor level (Figure 6.7). There is barely enough room for six people to sit one beside the other—and only provided that everyone puts their shopping bags on the floor. Because of its importance via its scarcity, it is not surprising that conflicts arise over the use of this seating area. Soon after the building opened, Philip Schneider wrote to Trump complaining that the marble bench was completely covered with flowerpots, prohibiting anyone from sitting there. Schneider also asked when the upper terraces were going to open. He added that the planning department "has not received a written reply concerning the four missing trees in the lobby of the Atrium that are required by the special permit as explained in Mr. Tenant's [sic] letter of March 7, 1984."[29] A response came explaining the need for flowerpots on the bench and signed with best wishes from Donald Trump himself: "we have had tremendous difficulties with respect to the bench—drug addicts, vagrants, et cetera have come to the Atrium in large numbers to sit and, in fact, to sleep on this bench." Trump added that the bench was even being "used for business purposes" and that "all sorts of 'horrors' had been taking place that effectively ruined the beautiful ambiance of a space which everyone loves so much."[30]

Figure 6.6. (*left*) One of the upper-level POPS, 2002.
Figure 6.7. (*below*) The only bench on the ground floor of the Trump POPS, 2002.

The "business purposes" to which Trump referred were not in themselves illegal. Quite the contrary: a *New York Times* article reported on these business activities on April 17, 1984: "Sylvia Heisel and Marc Lieberman run a dress company called Post Modern Productions Inc. The name sounds big, but the company is so small that it operates out of their apartments—hers on the East Side and his on the West. Casting about for an office in between, they struck on using one of the public atriums blossoming in the midtown buildings."[31] The pair's search for a place to work in midtown reads like a contemporary *Goldilocks and the Three Bears*. They found the IBM Atrium to be "too cold and drafty," the Olympic Tower "too dark and uncomfortable," the Park Avenue tables "hard to write on." Then they finally found "the perfect spot": the marble bench in the Trump Tower lobby. At that time there was a pianist there, so the two had music as well. The coworkers returned to their meeting spot one day to find that it had been covered with flowerpots. Lieberman commented that "[i]t was kind of a shock. . . . Have you ever tried to sit on a chrysanthemum?" They did not complain about the change because they "figured it was just the two of us against Trump." The same *New York Times* article reported that a Trump spokesman said that the flowers were not there to keep people off of the bench, rather "to soften up the vast expanse of marble, to give it some color and warmth."[32]

Today, the bench is chrysanthemum-free, but hardly inviting. Sitting on this bench opposite the gleaming elevators, one gets the sense of feeding from the margins of Trump's success. Tucked next to a T display case with images of properties few can afford, those seated on the bench recede against the wall. Actually, all of the Trump spaces are marginal to the building. They are literally tucked in strange corners, like the "parks," or hidden, like the bathrooms and telephones. Or one feels marginal occupying them, like the lobby/hallway that is too narrow for loitering, or the bench, on which one appears to be waiting for an appointment with the baron. Trump's repeated attempts to "secure" the bench are particularly hard to swallow, given that this paltry amenity sits at the physical juncture most crucial to Trump's Fifth Avenue subdistrict windfall: the link between the retail spaces that ring the atrium and the retail district outside the building.

Trump made even more money from the tower because of the many arms of his hydra-like corporation. For example, as the building's general manager, Trump collected a commission of $11 million on the sale of the forty-two floors of apartments. The Trump Organization, Trump's management and construction wing, collects an undisclosed amount for building

**132**

maintenance. Trump also sued the city to receive tax abatements for the property. These tax abatements were set up by the city to transform "under-utilized property" into low to moderate-income housing. Trump's apartments were selling in the early 1980s for from $500,000 to $3 million.[33]

Trump also received bonuses for building a "mixed use" building, or, as he called it, "the multiple use concept. . . . It's going to have some great retail stores, then office building floors where people work industriously, then exquisite living on the higher floors. Work, shopping, living together. That's what New York is all about."[34] But as the case of the disappearing bench indicates, only certain kinds of working, shopping, and living fit in with the Trump Tower concept. While providing retail services close to public spaces was a design idea championed by urbanists like William H. Whyte, it is hard to imagine that Trump Tower's retail zones serve a public purpose. Trump's assertion that his building is mixed-use strikes a false chord. The people who work in the building are not the people who live in the building or, for the most part, the people who shop in the building.[35] The people working at Avon do not make enough to pay $24,000 for an Asprey alligator handbag or $10,000 for a pair of diamond earrings. The people who work in Asprey do not make enough money to live in Trump Tower.

Though most midtown workers cannot afford to live in Trump Tower or shop in its boutiques, they might sometimes have lunch at the café on the basement level. The prices are high compared with other lunch spots, but other lunch spots don't have seating near the base of a marble waterfall (Figure 6.8). Looking over the railing of the ground floor at lunchtime, one finds the café tables crowded with brown trays, like the food court of a typical shopping mall. But this is not a food court or a café. Anyone can sit there, even if they do not purchase food. This fact is difficult to discern from the architectural clues.

If you venture downstairs you might locate—though it won't be easy—the greatest hidden amenity in Trump Tower: its bathrooms. Visitors do not happen upon them; I knew of their existence only by reading a list of the required amenities for the site. The ground floor also has a newsstand with souvenirs and a Tower Records. Neither of these shops borders the main atrium or is at all visible from the street or the main level. That said, people who frequent Trump Tower at lunch might find them and shop there.

The aesthetic aura of Trump Tower includes the visitors themselves. We all look out of place there (Figure 6.9). Our backpacks and plaid shorts in the summer and our fogged glasses and bulky coats in the winter only

seem to heighten the divide between what Trump is selling and how we are living. We all look a little overweight and overburdened without the protection of our living-room couch, from which we can laugh at Trump's escapades and the idiocy of his apprentices-to-be.

The real audience for the lavishness of the interior of Trump Tower is not the average New Yorker wandering through on his or her lunch break, or the visitor looking for a pay phone (which is also hidden in the basement). Rather, Trump Tower, like all the other members of the Trump real estate family, works as a set. It reinforces the product and its particular value. Like Minksoff, the owner of 590 Madison Avenue, Donald Trump makes money by selling real estate. Trump uses ideas of luxury and wealth to advertise and sell his real estate. His advertising, his personal image, and the aesthetic of his buildings project a public relations image of being over the top. Within Trump Tower, displays showcase Trump's other projects, including his ownership rights for the Miss Teen USA, Miss USA, and Miss Universe pageants, which Trump refers to at his Web site as "a suite of Trump Entertainment properties."[36]

Figure 6.8. (*left*) Seating area on lower level and waterfall, 2001
Figure 6.9. (*below*) Visitors at Trump Tower looking out over atrium and waterfall, 2003.

In 1990 Trump tried unsuccessfully to block the release of his personal financial information by the New Jersey Casino Control Commission. The

commission obtained the figures because it was involved in the review of a debt-restructuring plan that Trump had negotiated. Trump's numbers indicated that he was worth far less than he claimed, and that if banks had not restructured his debt he would have been overdrawn by $73.4 million by the end of the year. As the *New York Times* has reported, Trump's outlandish personal spending shone through the numbers. Before negotiations over his debt restructuring occurred, he had planned to spend nearly $500,000 a month on personal and household expenses. But his agreement with the banks led him to cut that number down to $450,000 during the first year, and weaned him down to $300,000 in two years' time. It is unsurprising but perhaps ironic that Donald Trump went to such lengths to block the public release of his private financial information because—as evidenced in the Trump Tower deal—his fortune was so solidly based on public money.

## Public Investment in Private Space

Following the launch of *The Apprentice*, the shop in the Trump Tower basement window was packed with "You're Fired" T-shirts. More recently, the gossip column in the *New York Daily News* reported that Trump's high-rent tenants and neighbors objected to the giant "You're Fired" sign that Trump hung from his building. Trump claimed to have not heard any complaints and countered that since the show was number one, it was "great for them." The reporter commented that the show was actually rated number six and that Asprey and Fendi probably were not benefiting from these ratings. He asked Trump, "what about all the money and effort that went into establishing and promoting brands such as Asprey and Avon?" "A lot of people would like to have my brand," Trump retorted.[37] Asprey invested an unprecedented $2,000 per square foot to build its store in Trump Tower in order to showcase its luxury goods.[38] In 2002 it was reported that Asprey was paying around $1,200 per square foot in rent.

Instead of sending his aspirants out to sell lemonade, perhaps Trump should set up more true-to-life business tests. He could see which team could use more public money to bolster private profits. Or contestants could team up with law students to see how much money they could make by suing other private entities to force them to pay their taxes. Contestants might consult an article written by Arlene Holpp Scala and Jean Levitan, two professors at William Patterson University, on how to teach students about class differences and debt:

"Living within one's means," an expression often carrying some judgmental overtones, requires increasing income and/or decreasing expenses. Living beyond one's means—having the buying power to initially develop "credit"—and then developing debt, provides an opportunity to examine class differences. Students can contrast the debt of someone like Donald Trump with his continued borrowing power against that of their peers, who develop debt resulting from credit cards and student loans. Discussing other ways to "legally" increase income facilitates further discussion of privilege.[39]

At the opening ceremony for Trump Tower, Mayor Ed Koch was asked by a reporter if he thought that it was right that the current construction boom in New York featured only office buildings, hotels, and luxury condominiums—implying that other projects might better serve the public good. Koch retorted, "Those are with private funds, aren't they? . . . And in America, if you have your own dollars you're allowed to build what you want."[40] But what the Trump case clearly demonstrates is that the funds for his building were not only private. Trump could not have built as he did without large public investment. This investment is not only illegible in the building's final design, but is also masked by the building's aesthetic of private grandeur. And those whose tax dollars were spent on building the Trump Tower are made to feel lucky to enjoy a taste of Trump's largesse. It is no wonder that employees of the Department of City Planning took it upon themselves to walk through Trump Tower on their way home from work to make sure that Trump was in compliance. But it is also no surprise that many visitors to Trump Tower are joyful about their experience. Trump Tower is considered one of the best of the POPS. And while the Department of City Planning has successfully fought both for better compliance and for increased signage indicating the "public" nature of the spaces, it is hard to see beyond all the brass, marble, and Ts. As Ada Louise Huxtable noted in her article published while the final designs for Trump Tower had yet to receive full city approval, "until the zoning law is changed or modified . . . we will continue to get what (builders) give us."[41] The aesthetics of Trump Tower resulted from a combination of incentive zoning programs ostensibly set up to create public benefit. We get the public that builders build for. In the case of Trump Tower, it is a public out of place, on the verge of overstaying or overstepping, frumpy, an unwelcome foreground to Trump's background of opulence and excess, and an unwitting underwriter of Trump's private fortune.

# Epilogue
## After 9/11

**Public spaces are constantly changing.** New regulations, changes in design, litigation outcomes, economic shifts, and new demands all affect the public nature of public space. Each of this book's chapters described controversies that took place mainly in the 1980s and 1990s. If public space and the idea of public space are constantly in flux, do the ideas raised in these cases still hold true fifteen years later? Research and writing of this book took place between 1999 and 2005: the two years before and four years after the destruction of the World Trade Center towers. How does a book on New York City written in the years after 9/11 take into account the impact of 9/11?

We should begin by asking what the phrase "after 9/11" might mean, since 9/11 refers both to a catastrophic event and to the date on which the event occurred. That the date in time was chosen to represent the event as opposed to its location—Pearl Harbor, Oklahoma City, Columbine—implies that life was one way before and was irrevocably another way afterward; that *everything* in New York was rendered instantly and totally different.

We are still trying to understand how 9/11 affected those who survived, the families of those who died, and those who worked during the arduous months of cleanup.[1] For those who lived in Lower Manhattan, the weeks and months following 9/11 involved not only the memories of the horrific day but also the inconvenience of not being allowed back in their apartments. When they were allowed back in their homes, they had to deal with the ash, smell, and noise of the cleanup.[2] It has been estimated that in comparison with 9/11 the subsequent invasions of Afghanistan and Iraq have resulted in at least 40,000 more deaths and countless more injuries, displacements, and losses of livelihood.

But how has public space in New York changed? Assigning causality to an event while its effects continue to unfold is nearly impossible. We must try to identify which changes were the direct result of the bombing of the World Trade Towers, which were the result of policies put in place in response to the bombing, and which were the result of processes put in place before 9/11. The short answer to the question is that public space in New York after 9/11 has changed not at all and completely.

If you today visited any one of the six case-study spaces, over six years after the destruction of the World Trade Center towers, it would be difficult to find any differences from how they're described in this book. We might expect the most changes at City Hall and at Jacob Javits Plaza: one site the seat of government for the city of New York, and the other the main office building for the U.S. federal government in New York. After 9/11, both were considered potential terrorist targets. Questions of security and safety were key issues in their stories and were used as justification for framing what could happen there.

At City Hall, security was used as a justification for former mayor Giuliani to limit the size of press conferences and demonstrations. At Federal Plaza, security concerns led to arguments against the presence of *Tilted Arc*. But both these sites look much the same today as they did during the 1980s and 1990s. In fact, before 9/11 both spaces were *already* under heightened security because of the bombing of the Federal Building in Oklahoma City in 1995 and because of the bombings in Sudan and Afghanistan by the United States in 1998. The current security configuration at City Hall, put in place in 1998, closed City Hall to the public, unless you were there for a meeting or a public hearing.

Times Square has changed radically since the summer of 2001. New "spectacular" billboards and entire buildings have gone up. It has certainly not "broken-in" as Kalman thought it would; if anything, Times Square looks brighter and cleaner than ever. After 9/11, city police indicated that Times Square, like Federal Plaza and City Hall, was a potential terrorist target. We might expect that security, especially on New Year's Eve, would have been tightened as a result. However, security on New Year's Eve in 2001 was at the same level as it was two years earlier for the millennium celebration. The millennium celebration security plan, code-named "Archangel," was "three years in the making," included methods for responding to chemical and biological attacks, and involved 8,000 police officers and six police helicopters, which monitored the event from above.[3]

At IBM there is a different set of sculptures on display than there was in the fall of 2001, but everything else seems the same.[4] Across the street at Sony Plaza, BB is still chatting with kids waiting in line to enter the Wonder Lab. Life at Sony Plaza continued without much interruption after 9/11.[5]

Of the three POPS, Trump Tower is the only one where security visibly increased after 9/11. The men in suits, who have always stood in front of the elevators, may now check your bags. But since most people don't realize that the elevators lead to additional public spaces (and not just the board room or Trump's luxury suite), the additional security may not impact the use of this space or its perception as public at all.

The ongoing stories of the case-study sites show little difference in the way public spaces are conceived of, managed, and regulated after the destruction of the World Trade Center (WTC). Instead, they follow the patterns of economic, social, and political forces at work well before 9/11. But what about Ground Zero itself? Does the unfolding history of the WTC site and its redevelopment process indicate shifts in how public space is thought of, planned for, and created? Does it point to new ways in which public spaces might be the sites and subjects of active public spheres?

Certainly the potential public of the WTC is without precedent. It is diverse and enormous. If the public of the WTC includes anyone with an interest in what happens there and how it happens, then the potential public is vast, extending far beyond the survivors, the victims' families, the people who live and work in the adjacent neighborhoods, the workers who cleared the site, New Yorkers, and Americans. The scale of the event and the global implications of the U.S. response to the attack stretch the very definition of the public to its limits.

For a time, it seemed that the WTC site—owned by a quasi government body and leased to a real estate developer—had become public through shared tragedy. As expansive as the potential and actual public of the WTC is, that public has already been framed. They have been framed by the public processes of decision making and by the design and management of the site itself. New Yorker's genuine concern for the shape their city would take, expressed through rich and difficult questions, was met with a series of closed competitions, symbolic meetings, and mediocre designs.

Even a cynical observer, noting the complicated brew of public, semi-public, and private stakeholders involved and the huge sums of money at stake, might have expected that the millions of eyes watching would have prompted the Lower Manhattan Development Corporation (LMDC) to involve at least some fraction of those who would live with, live in, work in, pass through, and see the project. What could have been an opportunity for developing active public spheres around this place along with discussions about how built form, aesthetics, politics, and economics shape public life even in quasi public and private spaces became instead a jump to design form. The unfolding stories of redevelopment signal that the process has been guided by forces set up before 9/11—patterns of ownership and control based on values of property and rent—and these forces are so intractable that even focused public attention can do little to shift them.

If the process has defined the WTC public as nonvoting judges in an architectural beauty contest, codes of conduct that govern the site itself limit their ability to act there. In the days and months after 9/11, New Yorkers and visitors to the city made shrines out of pictures, poems, flowers, and candles that created a constellation of markers of shared grief and memory. Some who travel to the WTC site expect to see the same kind of constant outpouring, perhaps less intense with the passing of time but still there. Instead they find signs on the fences forbidding small memorials of any kind. The criminalization of spontaneous memorials framed the public as consumers rather than producers of WTC histories. We can no longer represent our own memories and questions. Instead we read the boards on the fences around Ground Zero that define what happened that day. What could possibly be of such compelling government interest that expressions of grief should be criminalized? What is it about the aesthetic experience of these places—one as a neighborhood of small memorials and tokens, and one as a construction site with an already completed history—that makes them wholly incompatible?

The Port Authority has divided the site into locations where expressive activity is allowed. If you are part of a group of twenty-five or more people, you must submit in person an application for a permit for an expressive activity no more than seven days before and no less than thirty-six hours before the expressive activity is to take place. All participants must wear badges that list the location and time they are permitted to exercise their right to free speech. The badge must be worn on the "upper left breast of the outermost garment" and must "be clearly visible at all times."[6] The public has been constrained at the WTC through the design process, in codes of conduct, and in limits on expression. All these controls are reminiscent of the case-study stories. As others have commented, the WTC story is not completely different from past events, but more of the same.

The case-study sites themselves remain largely unchanged since 9/11. The processes that frame the WTC public are reminiscent of those processes at work in the case-study sites. It would seem that nothing about public space in New York has changed since 9/11. But in another way, everything about public space has changed since 9/11—at the WTC site, the case-study sites, and all over the United States. Six weeks after the destruction of the WTC towers, the public and therefore public space in New York and across the country was completely transformed. This transformation was not a direct result of the destruction of the WTC towers; rather, it was the direct result of laws enacted as part of the Patriot Act.

The possibility of public spaces becoming the sites and subjects of active public spheres has narrowed because we the public have been fundamentally altered. Active public spheres require accountability to function; the Patriot Act strips government accountability from what were Americans' most fundamental rights. The Patriot Act compromises rights to speech, association, privacy, and due process. People can be imprisoned indefinitely without being formally charged. Phone calls, e-mails, bank records, library records, medical histories, travels, Internet usage, and the contents of homes and offices are no longer private. The Patriot Act public is framed by the law itself and by the rhetoric backing it up. If people have nothing to hide, why should they be concerned about being watched? Such concern, in the rhetoric of "protection," belies guilt.

The Patriot Act thwarts efforts to remake public spaces by practicing democracy. Police officers now disguise themselves as protesters, carrying signs and shouting slogans. They carry two-way radios in backpacks and videotape crowds while marching as demonstrators. They not only gather information on people participating in the demonstrations, but in at least one case, their actions have directly influenced what happened at an event. During the Republican National Convention in New York in 2004, an undercover police officer infiltrated a march that was organized in support of poor and homeless people. When the officer was "arrested," onlookers shouted,

"Let him go." Police officers in riot gear responded to the protests by pushing against the crowd. This incident resulted in the arrest of at least two other people.[7]

Professional landscape architects and urban designers come under increased scrutiny in the post-9/11 security state. Our very work is suspect. We are on FBI lists of "scientific and technological experts" whose presence at U.S. border crossings triggers special checks. Our knowledge of cities and urban infrastructure, our ability to read plans and interpret spaces make us potentially dangerous. The fact that our knowledge base is considered potentially criminal should give designers pause to consider what we are capable of, to take seriously our power to shape public spaces and publics, and to rethink the way we imagine, represent, and create new urban futures.

# Notes

## Introduction

1. POPS are governed by the New York City Plaza Bonus Zoning Ordinance. The New York City Zoning Resolution was first developed in 1961. It allowed developers to build additional stories on their buildings if they provided a "public space" either outside or inside the building. Each space is governed by a contract between the developer/owner and the Department of City Planning. In 2000 the Department of City Planning, Jerold Kayden, and the Municipal Arts Society of New York published summaries of the contracts for all existing POPS, and the laws governing the spaces. For a description of the history of the program and an accounting of the spaces themselves see Jerold S. Kayden, New York Department of City Planning, and Municipal Art Society of New York, *Privately Owned Public Space: The New York City Experience* (New York: John Wiley, 2000).

2. The work of Nancy Fraser on the public sphere underlies my own understanding of the concept, in particular her critique of Jürgen Habermas. See Nancy Fraser, "Rethinking the Public Sphere," in *Habermas and the Public Sphere,* ed. Craig J. Calhoun (Cambridge, Mass.: MIT Press, 1992). Fraser's work on transnational public spheres has important implications for understanding the neoliberal city where public-private partnerships for the provision of public services situate private corporations within the matrix of the public sphere. The public sphere, notes Fraser,

"designates a theater in modern society in which political participation is enacted through the medium of talk. It is the space in which citizens deliberate about their common affairs, hence, an institutionalized arena of discursive interaction . . . a site for the production and circulation of discourses that can in principle be critical of the state . . . [it is] also conceptually distinct from the official economy; it is not an arena of market relations but rather one of discursive relations, a theater for debating and deliberating rather than for buying and selling" (2).

3. See, for example, work on Business Improvement Districts, such as Sharon Zukin, *The Cultures of Cities* (Cambridge, Mass.: Blackwell, 1995); on the expulsion of homeless people from sidewalks, streets and parks, and gated communities, such as Setha M. Low, *Behind the Gates: Life, Security, and the Pursuit of Happiness in Fortress America* (New York: Routledge, 2003); on the sale of community gardens, such as Lynn Staeheli, Don Mitchell, and Kristina Gibson, "Conflicting Rights to the City in New York's Community Gardens," *GeoJournal* 58, no. 2–3 (2002); and on public-private partnerships that manage public spaces such as Central Park. This litera-ture parallels studies on corporate involvement in public schools, prisons, security, and war.

4. See Setha Low's examination of two Costa Rican plazas in *On the Plaza: The Politics of Public Space and Culture* (Austin: University of Texas Press, 2000). Low's study includes a description of the social and political factors that led to the redesign of both plazas and of how the new designs were received by the people who used the spaces every day.

5. I use the term *aesthetics* to describe the sensory experiences resulting from a particular environment. This definition is related to the work of Susan Buck-Morss, in particular her understanding of the physicality and politics of aesthetics. Susan Buck-Morss, "Aesthetics and Anaesthetics: Walter Benjamin's Artwork Essay Recon-sidered," *October* 62 (Fall 1992).

6. "PPS's mission is to create and sustain public places that build communities. It operates programs based on transportation, parks, plazas and civic squares, public markets, community institutions, and public buildings. Since the organization's founding in 1975, PPS staff have worked in more than 1,000 communities, both within the U.S. and abroad, to help grow public spaces into vital community places—with programs, uses, and people-friendly settings that highlight local assets, spur social and economic rejuvenation, and serve community needs. In improving these public environments, PPS focuses on creating places that enrich people's experience of public life, through their distinctive identities and their integration into the com-munity fabric." Project for Public Spaces, *How to Turn a Place Around: A Handbook for Creating Successful Public Spaces* (New York: Project for Public Spaces, 2000), 11.

7. Project for Public Spaces, *How to Turn a Place Around*, 14, 15.

8. Mele's work is one example among many studies on how "[s]patial mean-ings are actively manipulated by the city and the state to represent diverse political

and economic agendas." Christopher Mele, *Selling the Lower East Side: Culture, Real Estate, and Resistance in New York City* (Minneapolis: University of Minnesota Press, 2000), 239.

9. Connections between economics, geography, and representation in American cities have been mapped by several scholars. See, for example, Sharon Zukin, *Landscapes of Power: From Detroit to Disney World* (Berkeley: University of California Press, 1991); David Harvey, *The Urban Experience* (Baltimore: Johns Hopkins University Press, 1989); Andy Merrifield, *Dialectical Urbanism: Social Struggles in the Capitalist City* (New York: Monthly Review Press, 2002); and Neil Smith, *Uneven Development: Nature, Capital, and the Production of Space* (Cambridge, Mass.: Blackwell, 1991).

10. Stephen Carr, Mark Francis, Leanne G. Rivlin, and Andrew M. Stone, eds. *Public Space* (New York: Cambridge University Press, 1992), 19–20.

11. Lynda Schneekloth and Robert Shibley, *Placemaking: The Art and Practice of Building Communities* (New York: John Wiley and Sons, 1995), 5.

12. See recently edited volumes, including Marcel Hénaff and Tracy B. Strong, *Public Space and Democracy* (Minneapolis: University of Minnesota Press, 2001); Andrew Light and Johnathan M. Smith, eds., *The Production of Public Space* (Oxford, England: Rowman and Littlefield, 1998); and Luc Nadal's dissertation "Discourses of Urban Public Space, U.S.A. 1960–1995: A Historical Critique" (Columbia University, 2000), which presents a comprehensive summary of the changing use of the term "public space."

13. The legal aspects of public space are complex. Actually, there is no *legal* definition of public space at all. Rather, the concept of the public realm as it relates to civil liberties such as free speech and state transportation laws regarding the management of public thoroughfares form the basis for much of the litigation surrounding the use of public space in New York. (Christopher Dunn, in discussion with the author, November 2000).

14. Don Mitchell, *The Right to the City: Social Justice and the Fight for Public Space* (New York: Guildford, 2003), 129.

15. In a lecture presented as part of the CUNY Politics and Public Space conference in November 2001, Cindy Katz describes the political implications of the management of Central Park by a nonprofit conservation organization that can raise money for the sole purpose of its own maintenance outside of the city budget. Money is raised from wealthy property owners around the park who have an interest in keeping the park clean and well maintained. Parks in other parts of the city have no such patrons. As tax money that would support park maintenance has been removed from the larger city budget, those who visit Central Park believe that everything is "all right" and enough tax money is being spent. The park's good maintenance gives the impression that the democratic system, and in particular the system that collects and spends tax dollars, is working well. This impression is based on the illusion that Central Park is still part of a larger system of money spent evenly across the city.

16. This chapter is based on a previously published article. Kristine Miller, "Art or Lunch: Designing a Public for New York's Federal Plaza," in *The Geography of Law: Landscape, Identity, and Regulation*, ed. William Taylor (London: Hart Publishing, 2005).

17. This chapter is based on a previously published article. Kristine Miller, "Condemning the Public: Design and New York's New 42nd Street," *GeoJournal* 58, no. 2–3 (2002).

18. This chapter follows on the work of recent scholarship on the transformation of Times Square, including Lynne B. Sagalyn, *Times Square Roulette: Remaking the City Icon* (Cambridge, Mass.: MIT Press, 2001); Samuel R. Delany, *Times Square Red, Times Square Blue* (New York: New York University Press, 1999); and in particular Alexander J. Reichl, *Reconstructing Times Square: Politics and Culture in Urban Development*, (Lawrence: University Press of Kansas, 1999).

19. Kayden, New York Department of City Planning, and Municipal Art Society of New York, *Privately Owned Public Space*, 173.

20. Naomi Klein's idea of branding as a unique type of retail marketing tied to a broad range of transnational social issues underlies my own understanding of Sony Plaza. See Naomi Klein, *No Logo* (New York: Picador, 2000).

21. Sony's equivalent of the Pillsbury Doughboy, but with surveillance-camera eyes.


## 1. Public Space as Public Sphere

1. The current City Hall is actually New York's third. The first two were located even further to the south in Manhattan on Pearl Street and on Wall Street. Carol von Pressentin Wright, *New York: Atlas of Manhattan, Maps, and Plans,* 2nd ed. (New York: Norton, 1991), 150.

2. At least until 1916 it appears that McComb received almost full credit for the design. For a discussion of the controversy, see *Twenty-first Annual Report of the American Scenic and Historic Preservation Society, 1916, to the Legislature of the State of New York* (New York: J. B. Lyon Company, 1916).

3. Von Pressentin Wright, *New York*, 150.

4. Edith [last name illegible], "Portraits in New York's City Hall," *Antiques* [publication date unknown]. (A photocopy of this article was obtained from the New York City Hall Library with the author's name cut off and the publication date missing. I have been unable to ascertain full publication details.)

5. When renovations on City Hall's ceremonial Blue Room were completed in December 1998, Giuliani announced that Koch and Dinkins were going to be moved to the hallway outside the room. Lisa Rein, "Ed and Dave's Pix Shut Out at City Hall," *Daily News*, December 12, 1998.

6. Barry Schwartz, "Mourning and the Making of a Sacred Symbol: Durkheim and the Lincoln Assassination," *Social Forces* 70, no. 2 (1991): 343.

7. Ibid.

8. The same article argued that the solemnity of the event was disturbed by the "pitiful" condition of the park and in particular by the "bootblack and news stands" and other vendors that stood along the park paths.

9. *Twentieth Annual Report of the American Scenic and Historic Preservation Society, 1915, to the Legislature of the State of New York* (New York: J. B. Lyon Company, 1915).

10. "Flying Enterprise" (photograph), 1952, New York Municipal Archives.

11. "Carlson in By Air; Official Reception Awaits Him Today," *New York Times,* January 17, 1952.

12. Clyde Haberman, "City Opens Its Heart to Freed Hostages," *New York Times,* January 31, 1981.

13. Art Commission of the City of New York, *History of City Hall Exhibit Brochure,* 1984.

14. *Hague v. Committee for Industrial Organization, 307 U.S. 496 (1939).*

15. *Clark v. Community for Creative Non-Violence,* 468 U.S. 288, March 1, 1984.

16. Rudolph Giuliani was mayor of New York from 1993 to 2001.

17. A few of these battles related to charges that the city denied Housing Works government contracts because of their criticism of the mayor and the lawsuits that Housing Works brought against the city regarding the use of the front steps of City Hall. See, for example, *Housing Works, Inc. v. Giuliani,* 56 Fed. Appx. 530 (2003), *Housing Works, Inc. v. Turner,* U.S. District Court (2004).

18. Lynda Richardson, "Celebrating a Ruling: Aids Group Rallies on City Hall Steps," *New York Times,* July 22, 1998.

19. Rudolph W. Giuliani, "The Next Phase of Quality of Life: Creating a More Civil City" (New York: Archives of Rudolph W. Giuliani, 107th Mayor, 1998). The rest of the quotes in this paragraph are drawn from this speech.

20. For instance, by enforcing speed limits, raising taxi safety standards, enforcing bicycle safety laws, decreasing noise pollution, and punishing people who litter and write graffiti ("a city with an increasing amount of graffiti is a city in which the rights of its people are being disrespected. And conversely, a city with decreasing amounts of graffiti is a city in which the rights of people are being respected," Giuliani, "The Next Phase of Quality of Life"). Giuliani's near obsession with graffiti in this particular speech is interesting in the context of his larger body of work aimed at limiting speech, since it has been argued that graffiti, or more specifically writing and tagging, is a form of speech used by people who feel they would not be heard otherwise. See, for example, Joe Austin, *Taking the Train: How Graffiti Art Became an Urban Crisis in New York City,* (New York: Columbia University Press, 2001); and Jeff Chang, *Can't Stop, Won't Stop: A History of the Hip-Hop Generation,* (New York: St. Martin's Press, 2005).

21. NYCLU, *NYCLU First Amendment Cases against the Giuliani Administration,* October 9, 2001, http://www.nyclu.org/giuliani2001.html (accessed May 19, 2005).

22. *Housing Works, Inc. v. Safir,* 98 Civ. 4994 (HB) (1998), 1.

23. Cited in Benjamin Weiser, "Ban on Big Gatherings at City Hall Is Ruled Unconstitutional," *New York Times,* July 21, 1998.

24. An excerpt from the memorandum is included in the judge's summary: "Elected officials as well as private citizens are allowed to hold press conferences on the steps or in the vicinity of the steps. However, the size of the group is limited to 25 persons in addition to any press personnel in attendance. The rationale behind this policy are [sic] safety and security concerns." *Housing Works, Inc. v. Safir,* 2000, 2.

25. Christopher Dunn and Arthur Eisenberg, "Plaintiffs' Pretrial Memorandum," New York Civil Liberties Union, 1999.

26. Weiser, "Ban on Big Gatherings at City Hall Is Ruled Unconstitutional."

27. Archives of Rudolph W. Giuliani, *New York Yankees Celebration, City Hall, Tuesday, October 29, 1996,* http://www.nyc.gov/html/rwg/html/96/yankees1.html (accessed September 14, 2004).

28. Stephen Handelman, "New York Throws a Giant Party, Greatest Spectacle in the History of Sport, Boggs Says," *Toronto Star,* October 30, 1996.

29. Gail Collins, "Editorial Notebook: Scenes from the Yankees' Parade," *New York Times,* October 30, 1996.

30. In his speech during the celebration, the mayor aligned the Yankees and their victory with the city of New York and New Yorkers: "The New York Yankees are the greatest franchise in sports, and New York is the greatest city in the world—and the Capital of the World. Like New Yorkers themselves, this team plays best under pressure. . . . And their victory is an inspiration for all of us. It is a metaphor for a city whose people perform best under pressure. It is a metaphor for a city that is undergoing a great renaissance . . . George, in honor of the Yankees championship season, I am honored to present you and the entire team with an official proclamation naming Tuesday, October 29, 1996, as 'New York Yankees Day' in the City of New York." Archives of Rudolph W. Giuliani, *New York Yankees Celebration, City Hall, Tuesday, October 29, 1996.* Guiliani's celebration of physical strength and his desire to make sports champions representatives of the city makes more disturbing his marginalization of New Yorkers suffering from AIDS and HIV.

31. "The defendants' prior and current practice of allowing more than 25 people to participate in press conferences, without incident, undermines their factual claim that the 25 person limit is narrowly tailored to address safety and security concerns." *Housing Works, Inc. V. Safir,* 101 F. Supp. 2d 163, 2000.

32. During this month, Giuliani also rededicated the refurbished *Statue of Justice* atop City Hall's cupola. Archives of the Mayor's Press Office, "Mayor Giuliani Rededicates the Statue of Justice and Celebrates the Restoration of City Hall: New

Clock to Count New York Minutes Atop Landmark Building," October 14, 1998, http://www.nyc.gov/html/om/html/98b/pr477-98.html (accessed May 18, 2006).

33. The city distributed tickets for the event at City Hall through city agencies and groups that in turn distributed the tickets to individuals of their choosing. However, these tickets didn't have names attached to them and individual's identification was not checked at the event.

34. Dunn and Eisenberg, "Plaintiffs' Pretrial Memorandum."

35. The meeting was attended by police officials and by lawyers from the Office of Corporation Counsel and the NYPD.

36. Dunn and Eisenberg, "Plaintiffs' Pretrial Memorandum."

37. Ibid.

38. See *Housing Works, Inc. v. Safir,* 98 Civ. 4994 (November 24, 1998) (Housing Works II).

39. Lynda Richardson, "Police Keep Close Tabs on AIDS Marchers at City Hall," *New York Times,* December 2, 1998.

40. When Housing Works and the NYCLU first informed the Office of Corporation Counsel that they would seek a summary judgment, the counsel asked them to hold off for a few days, saying they would rewrite the policy. They did not, in fact, write a new policy.

41. Dunn and Eisenberg, "Plaintiffs' Pretrial Memorandum."

42. Ibid.

43. Between February 23—the day before the new policy was enacted—and March 15, 1999, the city permitted twelve or thirteen events to take place on the steps.

44. Dunn and Eisenberg, "Plaintiffs' Pretrial Memorandum."

45. The mayor and the police commissioner unevenly enforced even this policy. Councilwoman Christine Quinn was not allowed to hold on the front steps a press conference with community members to draw attention to the murder of a young gay man in Harlem. After she called on Council Speaker Peter Vallone to complain, Quinn was eventually allowed to hold the event. "The Mayor and the First Amendment," *New York Times,* November 16, 1999.

46. Dunn and Eisenberg, "Plaintiffs' Pretrial Memorandum."

47. *Housing Works, Inc. v. Safir,* 2000.

48. Dunn and Eisenberg, "Plaintiffs' Pretrial Memorandum."

49. Ibid.

50. Ibid.

51. Ibid.

52. Richardson, "Police Keep Close Tabs on AIDS Marchers at City Hall." Michael D. Hess, the city's corporation counsel, said there was never an agreement with the protest organizers over how many people would be allowed on the grounds. He said that since only 186 people showed up, the issue was moot.

53. Dunn and Eisenberg, "Plaintiffs' Pretrial Memorandum."

54. Ibid.

55. *Housing Works, Inc. v. Safir*, 2000.

56. For example, a court case heard in December 2000 gave Housing Works permission to use amplified sound in the plaza in front of City Hall *(Housing Works v. Kerik).* The city appealed, and in 2002, judges Minor and Leval in the U.S. Court of Appeals argued that the city could control sound amplification. But this decision is interesting for a different reason. While Judge Leval argued that the steps of City Hall are unarguably traditional public forum, Judge Minor argued that they were not, noting that even if they were, they ceased to be so in the summer of 1998 when the city closed them to the public for reasons of security. Judge Minor argued further that even though the steps were closed as a public forum, it should not preclude the mayor from holding whatever kind of event he wants to there. Minor added that the previous three judgments (Housing Works I, II, and III) were based on faulty logic, and said that he added this information to the case in the event that the Bloomberg administration wanted to entirely close the steps to outside speech.

57. The *New York Times* reported that the Housing Works settlement was the largest in a string of cases made by a variety of groups and individuals charging that senior officials in Giuliani's administration retaliated against them for criticism. The total cost to the city of those cases and the Housing Works cases totals nearly $7 million. See Jim Dwyer, "City to Pay AIDS Group in Settlement," *New York Times*, May 27, 2005.

58. Sander L. Gilman, *Disease and Representation: Images of Illness from Madness to AIDS* (Ithaca, N.Y.: Cornell University Press, 1988), 271.

59. Ibid., 271.

60. A study on American's perceptions of HIV/AIDS completed at the time of the City Hall controversy showed growing misinformation and the need for increased public awareness of the actualities of the disease: "55 percent of Americans believed in 1997 that they could be infected by sharing a drinking glass with an infected person, compared with 48 percent in 1991. Forty-one percent believed that AIDS might be contracted from a public toilet, compared with 34 percent in 1991, according to the survey by researchers at the University of California at Davis." Lynda Richardson, "World AIDS Day Seen Regaining Old Fervor," *New York Times*, November 28, 1998.

61. Lisa L. Colangelo, "World AIDS Day Brings Crisis Home," *New York Daily News*, December 2, 2003.

62. Smithsonian Institution National Museum of American History, *September 11: Bearing Witness to History*, http://americanhistory.si.edu/september11/collection/record.asp?ID=43 (accessed May 17, 2005).

63. I am thinking here of the work of artist Fred Wilson, and in particular his work at the Maryland Historical Society, where he removed a set of slave shackles from their original collection and reinstalled them in an exhibit of a silver serving set.

## 2. Art or Lunch?

1. In piecing together this ongoing history of Federal Plaza, this chapter draws upon several sources, including government correspondence and hearing testimonies relating to Richard Serra's *Tilted Arc* published in Clara Weyergraf-Serra and Martha Buskirk, *Richard Serra's Tilted Arc* (Eindhoven, Netherlands: Van Abbemuseum, 1988); Rosalyn Deutsche, *Evictions: Art and Spatial Politics* (Cambridge, Mass.: MIT Press, 1996); Douglas Crimp, "Art in the 80s: Myth of Autonomy," *Precis* 6 (1987); and Harriet Senie, *The Tilted Arc Controversy: Dangerous Precedent?* (Minneapolis: University of Minnesota Press, 2002).

2. The Pentagon is the largest.

3. "New Federal Office Building: A Capital in Microcosm," *New York Times,* August 29, 1968.

4. Weyergraf-Serra and Buskirk, *Richard Serra's Tilted Arc,* 124.

5. Maintaining the fountain proved to be difficult, though while it was working it was described as "something of a Mecca to what seems to be an increasing number of lunchtime eaters who bring food from home." "New Federal Office Building," *New York Times.* The same article also pointed out that upon the building's completion critics argued that the blank-concrete facade on Broadway was an eyesore and that parking, public transportation, and eating facilities were inadequate in light of the thousands of workers who were now concentrated in one area.

6. Paul Goldberger, "Critic's Notebook: Harmonizing Old and New Buildings," *New York Times,* May 2, 1985.

7. Damon Stetson, "Federal Employees Rally Here to Protest Delay in Pay Raise," *New York Times,* October 2, 1971.

8. Herbert Muschamp, *New York Times,* April 24, 1995, B1; Weyergraf-Serra and Buskirk, *Richard Serra's Tilted Arc.*

9. Robert Storr, "Tilted Arc: Enemy of the People?" *Art in America* (September 1985).

10. See Senie, *The Tilted Arc Controversy.*

11. Weyergraf-Serra and Buskirk, *Richard Serra's Tilted Arc,* 3.

12. Michael Kimmelman, "Abstract Art's New World, Forged for All," *New York Times,* June 7, 2005.

13. The *Tilted Arc* case has been featured in numerous articles related to the role of public art in public life, to government controls, and to art and expression. See, for example, Gregg M. Horowitz, "Public Art/Public Space: The Spectacle of the Tilted Arc Controversy," *Journal of Aesthetics and Art Criticism* 54, no. 1 (1996); Caroline Levine, "The Paradox of Public Art: Democratic Space, the Avant-Garde, and Richard Serra's *Tilted Arc," Philosophy and Geography* 5, no. 1 (2002); and Pilar Viladas, "Art for Whose Sake?" *Progressive Architecture* 65, no. 4 (1985).

14. Cited in Weyergraf-Serra and Buskirk, *Richard Serra's Tilted Arc,* 26.

15. Ibid., 45.

16. Ibid., 46.

17. Ibid., 47.

18. Ibid., 45–48.

19. Ibid., 113. As a result of these hearings and the GSA's press releases, the *Tilted Arc* debates quickly attracted national attention. In his *Newsweek* column, conservative commentator George F. Will weighed in, saying, "(s)ome Serra defenders say his First Amendment rights are being trampled. But the issue is not a person's right to 'express' his whims in rusty steel. The issue is the public's right not to be saddled with the results forever. Even if the public's hostility were just a whim, so what? Artists who peddle their whims as art, counting on an absence of critical standards, cannot suddenly claim to have standards superior to the public's and incomprehensible to the public. And they cannot hide behind this crashing non sequitur: great innovations in art often have met hostility, therefore whatever provokes hostility must be a great innovation. Joan Mondale says the public should give 'Tilted Arc' time to prove its 'eternity.' Sounds like a long wait." George F. Will, "Giving Art a Bad Name," *Newsweek*, September 16, 1985.

20. Cited in Weyergraf-Serra and Buskirk, *Richard Serra's Tilted Arc*, 126.

21. Ibid., 113.

22. Ibid., 128.

23. Ibid., 12.

24. Ibid., 223.

25. Ibid.

26. Ibid.

27. Ibid.

28. Tom Finkelpearl, *Dialogues in Public Art* (Cambridge, Mass.: MIT Press, 2000), 70.

29. Cited in Weyergraf-Serra and Buskirk, *Richard Serra's Tilted Arc*, 61.

30. Cited in Finkelpearl, *Dialogues in Public Art*, 26. Although Crimp's interview was published after Martha Schwartz's work was installed, the critic did not comment whether or not that design supported his definition of public space.

31. Cited in Weyergraf-Serra and Buskirk, *Richard Serra's Tilted Arc*, 26.

32. Ibid.

33. Ibid. In Crimp's definition of public space, a place is made public by its use by members of the public, regardless of whether or not they are using that site for speech acts or demonstrations.

34. Deutsche, *Evictions*.

35. Deutsche does not go into detail on the relationships between democracy and public space; that is, how democracy "happens" in public spaces. This question is taken up in the following chapter, which addresses space and the First Amendment.

36. Deutsche, *Evictions*, 259.

37. Ibid.

38. Elizabeth K. Meyer, *Martha Schwartz: Transfiguration of the Commonplace* (Washington, D.C.: Spacemaker Press, 1997).

39. John Beardsley, "The Haunting of Federal Plaza," *Landscape Architecture* 86, no. 5 (1996), 159.

40. Ibid., 159.

41. Cited in Finkelpearl, *Dialogues in Public Art*.

42. Beardsley, "The Haunting of Federal Plaza."

43. Weyergraf-Serra and Buskirk, *Richard Serra's Tilted Arc*.

44. "ASLA Awards 1997," *Landscape Architecture* 87, no. 11 (November 1997): 40–75.

45. "ASLA Awards 1997," 55.

46. Ibid., 54.

47. Meyer, *Martha Schwartz*, 149.

48. Clare Cooper-Marcus, "Statement vs. Design," *Landscape Architecture* 86, no. 11 (November 1996), 27.

49. In *The Social Life of Small Urban Spaces* (Washington, D.C.: Conservation Foundation, 1980), Whyte described the kinds of features that make a public plaza successful.

50. Cited in Finkelpearl, *Dialogues in Public Art*, 63.

51. Ying Chan, "The INS Waiting Game," *New York Daily News*, July 16, 1995; Austin Fenner, "Marchers Flood Downtown: 10,000 Protest Cop Slaying of African Vendor," *New York Times*, April 16, 1999.

52. Meyers, *Martha Schwartz*, 7–8.

53. Cited in Carrie Jacobs, "Que Serra, Serra," *New York Magazine*, January 20, 1997.

54. Christopher Dunn, in discussion with the author, November 2000.

55. Cited in Weyergraf-Serra and Buskirk, *Richard Serra's Tilted Arc*, 75.

56. Susan Sachs, "Guiliani's Goal of Civil City Runs into First Amendment," *New York Times*, July 6, 1998.

57. Crimp, "Art in the 80s," 75.

## 3. Condemning the Public in the New Times Square

1. The boundaries of the Times Square Business Improvement District include portions of blocks, and dip in and out of the blocks between Eighth and Ninth avenues and Broadway and Sixth Avenue.

2. Alexander J. Reichl, *Reconstructing Times Square: Politics and Culture in Urban Development* (Lawrence: University Press of Kansas, 1999), 44.

3. Reichl's book is a thorough documentation of the redevelopment process through 1998. Reichl describes and analyzes what was an incredibly complex process, including numerous governmental and private interests.

4. This paper does not discuss historic-preservation organizations and their role in redevelopment. However, it is interesting to note that preservation in Times Square was limited to a few historic theaters, including the New Amsterdam. Disney uses the New Amsterdam to show live performances of its films. For more information on Disney in Times Square and on historic preservation, see Reichl, *Reconstructing Times Square.*

5. Reichl discusses the efforts of the Municipal Arts Society (MAS) to block plans for four large, white office towers designed by architect Philip Johnson. MAS displayed computer-generated images of how the office towers would dwarf surrounding buildings. Reichl, *Reconstructing Times Square,* 145.

6. Once taken, the state can then sell the land to another private owner.

7. Section 101 of the New York Consolidated Laws states: "It is the purpose of this law to provide the exclusive procedure by which property shall be acquired by exercise of the power of eminent domain in New York state; to assure that just compensation shall be paid to those persons whose property rights are acquired by the exercise of the power of eminent domain; to establish opportunity for public participation in the planning of public projects necessitating the exercise of eminent domain; to give due regard to the need to acquire property for public use as well as the legitimate interests of private property owners, local communities and the quality of the environment, and to that end to promote and facilitate recognition and careful consideration of those interests; to encourage settlement of claims for just compensation and expedite payments to property owners; to establish rules to reduce litigation, and to ensure equal treatment to all property owners."

8. "In 1968, the New York State Urban Development Corporation Act (UDCA) was enacted for the express purposes of promoting a vigorous and growing economy, ameliorating blighted and deteriorating areas throughout the State, and supplying adequate and safe dwelling accommodations for families of low income." *Fannie Mae Jackson et al., Respondents-Appellants v. New York State Urban Development Corporation et al.,* 110 A.D.2d 304, 494 N.Y.S.2d 700, 1985, 2.

9. Reichl, *Reconstructing Times Square,* 98.

10. Ibid.

11. Oxford English Dictionary, 2nd ed., s.v. "blight."

12. For more information on the relationships between language, metaphor, and displacement, see Tim Cresswell, "Weeds, Plagues, and Bodily Secretions: A Geographical Interpretation of Metaphors of Displacement," *Annals of the Association of American Geographers* 87, no. 2 (1997).

13. Barbara Goldstein, "Constructivism in LA," *Village Voice,* September 1, 1998.

14. The Times Square Business Improvement District's *Report on the Secondary Effects of the Concentration of Adult Use Establishments in the Times Square Area* did not draw a direct correlation between the presence of adult-use establishments and street crime.

15. Reichl, *Reconstructing Times Square*, 98.

16. It is important to note that the legislative process that approved the use of eminent domain in Times Square is now defunct. The Board of Estimate was dismantled in the 1989 City Charter. Eminent domain cases are now heard by the City Council (Reichl, *Reconstructing Times Square*, 189). Interestingly, the reason for the dismantling of the Board of Estimate was that the Supreme Court deemed it unconstitutional because it conflicted with the one-person, one-vote rule. However, once legislative bodies have deemed a project to be in the public interest, courts rarely rule against these decisions. Defendants in eminent domain cases cite *Berman v. Parker* (1954), "in which the Supreme Court established the now-familiar principle that courts will not second guess the decision of local governments in land use and redevelopment." *Rosenthal & Rosenthal, Inc. v. New York State Urban Dev. Corp.*, 771 F.2d 44; U.S. App. (1985).

17. Sagalyn, 383–84.

18. Johnson and Burgee were responsible for the design of the AT&T Building, which will be discussed in chapter 5.

19. "Vibrancy to Vacancy: Remaking the Deuce," *New York Times*, August 9, 1992.

20. Peter Grant, "State Seeks New Plan for Times Square Revival," *Crane's New York Business*, August 3, 1992–August 9, 1992.

21. Peter Hall and Michael Bierut, eds., *Tibor Kalman: Perverse Optimist* (New York: Princeton Architectural Press, 1998), 58.

22. Ibid., 401.

23. Ibid., 59.

24. For a general critique of Kalman's work and its relationships to corporate interests, see Thomas Frank, "Thomas Frank on Tibor Kalman: Half Empty," *Artforum* 37, no. 6 (1999).

25. Cited in Hall and Bierut, eds., *Tibor Kalman*, 402.

26. For a discussion of public art and the transformation of Times Square, see Julie Ault, "Public Art," 1996, http://www.undo.net/cgi-bin/openframe.pl?x=/Facts/Eng/fault.htm (accessed June 11, 2005).

27. There are, however, important differences. For example, in the drawings the neon signs are present but their messages indicate smaller-scale stores and theaters rather than the huge CBS and Disney tenants that occupy the same spaces today.

28. Cited in Hall and Bierut, eds., *Tibor Kalman*, 401.

29. "Keeping Times Square clean, safe and friendly" is part of the mission statement of the Times Square Business Improvement District, a private nonprofit that runs sanitation, security, and publicity services and is funded by a mandatory assessment on commercial buildings. See Reichl, *Reconstructing Times Square*, 154–55.

30. Neil Selkirk, *1000 on 42nd* (New York: PowerHouse Books, 2000), postscript.

31. Ibid., 1.

32. Ibid., afterword.

33. Cited in Hall and Bierut, *Tibor Kalman*, 77.

34. Disney's first stage production in the newly renovated New Amsterdam Theater was *Beauty and the Beast* (Reichl, *Reconstructing Times Square*, 157). Its storyline all but tells young girls that they can change violent men if they just love them enough. While this point seems obvious based on a cursory understanding of the movie's plot, a shocking misreading can be found in Francois Bovon's October 1999 article titled "The Child and the Beast: Fighting Violence in Ancient Christianity," published in the *Harvard Theological Review* 92, no. 4. Bovon states, "A contrasting theme to that of the violence in nature is presented in the successful Walt Disney movie *Beauty and the Beast*. . . . In the movie, the beast is slowly tamed by the beauty. At a precise moment, he overcomes his natural cruelty and opens his paw, which is now filled with grain, and delights in the birds who come to feed on it. The message is clear: such is the power of love" (369).

35. Cited in Dan Bischoff, "Signs of the Times," *Metropolis Magazine*, February–March 1998, 42.

36. Senator George D. Maziarz said, "For too many years the needs and shortcomings of Niagara Falls have been debated and discussed. With today's announcement it is clear that the time for endless circles of talk is over and the time for action has begun. By creating an entity whose sole focus is the development of Niagara Falls and using the successful Times Square redevelopment project as a model, I have great confidence that Governor Pataki's plan will help Niagara Falls turn the corner to finally realize its full potential." New York State Office of the Governor, "Governor Pataki Showcases 42nd St. Success Stories," June 14, 2001, http://www.state.ny.us/governor/press/year01/june14_7_01.htm (accessed April 7, 2005).

37. New York State Office of the Governor, "Governor Pataki Showcases 42nd St. Success Stories." If we need to discuss further Kalman's misreading of the effects of the market on urban development, we could look at suggestions for streamlining the eminent-domain process inspired by the Times Square transformation. The Group of 35, a committee appointed by Senator Schumer, published a report in June 2001 titled "Preparing for the Future: A Commercial Development Strategy for New York City." The report presented options for increasing large-scale office development and "a comprehensive blueprint of the actions that will be needed to ensure that New York City has enough space to accommodate anticipated future growth" (U.S. Senator Charles E. Schumer and Honorable Robert E. Rubin, "Preparing for the Future: A Commercial Development Strategy for New York," http://urban.nyu.edu/g35/Group-35.pdf [accessed May 28, 2007]). One of the report's main recommendations was that the city should make greater use of eminent domain in order to assemble "developable" parcels, and it cited the Times Square success as an example of how "the powers of eminent domain eliminates a number of the barriers to assemblage by compelling property owners to sell and severing the leases of existing tenants"

**158**

(41). The committee also recommended that the city use condemnation to remove "office site hold-outs." In cases where 85 percent of desired parcels have been acquired and the remaining 15 percent or less refuse to sell, development can proceed.

38. See Reichl, *Reconstructing Times Square*; Delany, *Times Square Red, Times Square Blue*; and Sagalyn, *Times Square Roulette*.

39. *West 41st Street Realty LLC et al. v. New York State Urban Development Corporation*, 2238, Supreme Court of New York Appellate Division, First Department, Lexis 11245, November 9, 2000.

40. Michael Sorkin, *Some Assembly Required* (Minneapolis: University of Minnesota Press, 2001).

41. The only thing remotely "leftist" about the Times Square transformation process was the fact that it involved so much state investment.

42. *Sugette Kelo, et al., Petitioners, v. City of New London, Connecticut, et al.*, 04-108, Supreme Court of the United States, 2005, U.S. Lexis 5011. Decided June 23, 2005.

## 4. Bamboozled?

1. Kayden, New York Department of City Planning, and Municipal Art Society of New York, *Privately Owned Public Space*, 23.

2. Ibid., 173.

3. Joseph Berger, "Strolling Hidden Nooks in Manhattan's Canyons," Midtown Journal, *New York Times*, March 11, 1991.

4. "The Municipal Art Society is a private, non-profit membership organization whose mission is to promote a more livable city. Since 1893, the MAS has worked to enrich the culture, neighborhoods and physical design of New York City. It advocates for excellence in urban design and planning, contemporary architecture, historic preservation and public art." Municipal Art Society of New York, "The Art of Making New York Livable," http://www.mas.org/home.cfm (accessed May 28, 2007).

5. Bruce Lambert, "Neighborhood Report, Midtown: Public Atria at the Heart of a Policy Debate," *New York Times*, November 19, 1995.

6. Some of the design elements of Paley Park can be found in the IBM Atrium. For example, both include trees planted in a grove with movable seating scattered below. Also, both spaces have a tranquil feeling, as if one is far removed from the city.

7. Berger, "Strolling Hidden Nooks in Manhattan's Canyons."

8. See New York Department of City Planning Special Permit C 770209 ZSM, New York Department of City Planning files.

9. IBM did not build to this limit. They used 92,052 square feet. However, as noted in Kayden, New York Department of City Planning, and Municipal Art Society of New York, *Privately Owned Public Space*, 68: "In some cases owners have used some

of the bonus floor area to which they are entitled not in their building but as a trade-in to obtain other benefits authorized by the Zoning Resolution such as excess tower coverage."

10. "The bonus multiplier for the Covered Pedestrian Space was increased by 1.5 sf above the basic rate of 11 sf for additional height of the space." New York City Department of City Planning, Public Space Record 515, 2002.

11. Revolving doors were added in 1985.

12. An article in *Crain's New York Business* noted that some of those against the proposal included city officials and members of the nonprofit world who were often on the pro rather than con side of battles for more art in city spaces.

13. Ivan C. Karp, OK Harris, to Joseph Rose, Department of City Planning, April 11, 1995.

14. The following year, Minskoff announced his proposal to redevelop Columbus Circle, and included as the major portion of the development a new corporate headquarters for Sotheby's.

15. At the time of writing, only one page of this report was available in the files of the Department of City Planning. The department is filing a Freedom of Information Act request, and the complete report should be available in June 2004.

16. Peter Rothschild and Charlotte Fahn, Parks Council, to Joseph Rose, City Planning Commission, September 11, 1995.

17. Ibid.

18. Municipal Art Society Planning Committee to the New York City Planning Commission on the proposed modification of 590 Madison Avenue's public garden, September 14, 1995. It is impossible to prove because it is impossible to see internal correspondence from Department of City Planning files, but IBM's diminishing care for the atrium may have been part of larger efforts to exclude the homeless from the space.

19. Carol Vogel, "Inside Art," *New York Times*, December 15, 1995.

20. Ken Smith, "Requiem for an Atrium," *Landscape Architecture*, April 1999, 4.

21. The ULURP process involves several steps, including a community board review, a community board public hearing, a borough president review, a City Planning Commission review, and a City Planning Commission public hearing, City Council review, and mayoral review.

22. The community board for the IBM Atrium is Community Board Five. It is one of fifty-nine community boards in New York City. Members of the community board are nonsalaried. They are appointed by the borough president and are officials of the city of New York. Kyle Merker, "Welcome to Community Board Five," 2004, http://www.cb5.org/role.php4 (accessed May 1, 2004).

23. Maurice Roers, in discussion with the author, March 20, 2004, and March 25, 2004.

24. Kayden, New York Department of City Planning, and Municipal Art Society of New York, *Privately Owned Public Space*, 302.

25. Ibid., 301.

26. Ibid., 301–2.

27. PaceWildenstein would have also been able to use expenses related to the exhibitions as tax write-offs.

28. Nicholas Fish to Edward J. Minskoff, November 10, 1995, Community Board Five files.

29. Ibid.

30. Ibid.

31. Melissa Harris to Lola Finkelstein, November 13, 1996, Community Board Five files.

32. Ibid.

33. Ruth Messinger to Richard Schaffer, July 27, 1992, Office of the President of the Borough of Manhattan archive.

34. Michael Presser to Richard Schaffer, July 13, 1992, Community Board Five files.

35. Richard Schaffer to Ruth Messinger, August 7, 1992, City Planning Commission of the City of New York archive.

36. David McGregor, "Urban Planning: Are the City's Public Plazas in Jeopardy?" *Newsday*, May 14, 1995.

## 5. Targeted Publics and Sony Plaza

1. Paul Goldberger, "Philip Johnson Is Dead at 98: Architecture's Restless Intellect," *New York Times*, January 27, 2005. This comment was written in an obituary celebrating Johnson's life. Earlier comments by Goldberger on the building were more critical. See Paul Goldberger, "Architecture View: Some Welcome Fiddling with Landmarks," *New York Times*, May 24, 1992.

2. Verena Dobnik, "Innovative, Influential Architect Philip Johnson Dies at Age 98," *Associated Press Worldstream*, January 26, 2005.

3. See Paul Betts, "AT&T to Hive Off 66% of Total Assets," *Financial Times*, January 9, 1982.

4. For example, Johnson's Glass House in Connecticut and his PPG Building in Pittsburgh.

5. Before his postmodern run, of which AT&T is arguably the pinnacle, Johnson's projects included working with his mentor Ludwig Mies van der Rohe on the Seagrams Building, New York's Museum of Modern Art Abby Aldrich Rockefeller Sculpture Garden, and the IDS Center in Minneapolis. He was awarded the 1979 Pritzker Prize, the most prestigious honor for an architect.

6. Johnson's comments may reveal more about his own bravado than recount

the facts. At the same time that Johnson argued he was actively pursued by AT&T, he asked the *New Yorker* to remove reference to his homosexuality from of an article the magazine was preparing on him "for fear of losing the commission for the AT&T Building." Christopher Hawthorne, "Philip Johnson, 1906–2005: America's Dean of Architects," *Los Angeles Times*, January 27, 2005.

7. "The Shape of Things to Come," *Economist*, March 5, 1988.

8. "Wheeling Out Baby Bell to Rattle IBM," *Economist*, November 14, 1981, 14.

9. Johnson described his client at AT&T as a "megalomaniac of proper proportions, a good 19th century buccaneer . . . that said I want the most monumental, I want a building that's entirely different from these glass boxes, I want something that will say to the world AT&T." Cited in New York City Planning Commission, *Excerpt of the Public Meeting of the City Planning Commission*, Item 22, Sony, August 5, 1992, 24. In a *New York Times* article on the remodel, Johnson lay part of the blame on AT&T: "AT&T was adamant—they wanted a Bernini kind of monumentality." Cited in David W. Dunlap, "Remaking Spaces for Public Use," *New York Times*, September 27, 1992.

10. New York City Planning Commission, *Resolution*, Calendar 1, C 841023 Zsm, September 24, 1984, 2.

11. New York City Planning Commission, Special Permit C 841023 Zsm, 1984, 3.

12. Infoquest went through a few overhauls to try to draw more people.

13. Carol von Pressentin Wright, *Blue Guide: New York*, 2nd ed. (New York: Norton, 1991), 392.

14. Ibid.

15. The redesign also met other needs for Sony, including accommodating an additional 600 employees.

16. Claudia H. Deutsch, "Carving Chippendale into the Sony Image," *New York Times*, February 21, 1993.

17. Klein, *No Logo*, 5.

18. Fraser makes this argument to counter Habermas's idea that in the public sphere, differences of status could be "bracketed" and that all participants would discuss issues as "peers." Fraser, "Rethinking the Public Sphere."

19. Kayden, New York Department of City Planning, and Municipal Art Society of New York, *Privately Owned Public Space*, 169.

20. Goldberger, "Architecture View."

21. Patricia McCobb, letter to the editor, August 12, 1992.

22. At the 1992 hearing, Sally Goodgold of the City Club of New York also criticized the commission for interpreting this change as minor, saying, "I hope that at no time in the future will this be minor whenever an inch of public space is taken away from the public." Goodgold also suggested that if Sony were allowed to keep the Jumbotron in the space, they could show public hearings that were

happening at City Hall. New York City Planning Commission, *Excerpt of the Public Meeting of the City Planning Commission*, 101–7. As mentioned in chapter 4, what constitutes major versus minor modifications continues to be an issue. At Sony, this issue was raised not only during the hearing regarding the proposed changes to the bonus spaces, but also in correspondence between Community Board Five and the City Planning Commission. See, for example, Michael Presser to City Planning Commission, July 17, 1992, New York Department of City Planning archive; and Richard Schaffer to Community Board Five, August 7, 1992, New York Department of City Planning archive.

23. New York City Planning Commission, *Excerpt of the Public Meeting of the City Planning Commission*, Item 22, Sony, August 5, 1992.

24. Ibid., 47–48.

25. Ibid., 26–27.

26. Ibid.

27. Ibid., 19.

28. Ibid. "We provide an equivalent area here because we give you a space that has more CPS and it generates a bonus of 117,000 square feet, an equivalent bonus, as opposed to 104,000 square feet before. . . . And what happens here is that we satisfy that quantitative standard, that's No. 1. So the equivalent bonus is higher."

29. Ibid., 113–17.

30. The race with Trump Tower is close, but Trump's amenities—such as the café, bathrooms, telephones, and tables and chairs—are all on a lower level, making them less apparent.

31. BB is a sort of hybridized feature from William Whyte's *Social Life of Small Urban Spaces.*

32. "At Sony Wonder Technology Lab, a four-story, hands-on science and technology center, you're not going to just see technology at work—you're going to be part of it! Personalize a swipe card at Log-in and explore communications technology as a Media Trainee. You'll be given the opportunity to create a unique musical composition, take a cyber-journey, look at the inner workings of innovative technology and experience High Definition in our 72-seat theater. You're sure to become a techno-wiz so be sure to pick up your graduation certificate at Log-out!" *Sony Wonder Technology Lab Brochure*, Sony Wonder Technology Lab, 2001.

33. This concern was expressed by members of Community Board Five and by members of the City Planning Commission. See, for example, Michael Presser, letter to the City Planning Commission, July 17, 1992, New York Department of City Planning archive.

34. Klein, *No Logo*, 150.

35. Herbert Sturtz to Donald Elliot, Esquire, July 12, 1984, New York City Planning Commission archive.

36. MTV Networks owns Nickelodeon.

37. "Nickelodeon and Epic Records Sign Home Video/Audio Deal," Business Wire, May 11, 1993.

38. Sony's use of stealth marketing has been documented. In one case, models were hired by the U.S. branch of Sony Ericsson Mobile Communications to sit in bars with Sony cell phones and strike up conversations with young men about how cool their new phone was and invite them to try it. In another case, Sony Ericsson hired actors to stand near New York City landmarks and ask people to take their picture using their Sony phone. See Suzanne Vranica, "Advertising: That Guy Showing Off His Hot New Phone May Be a Shill," *Wall Street Journal*, July 31, 2002.

39. For more on the "educational experience" of Sony Wonder, see Elizabeth Hanly, "Fast Forward: Visit the Sony Wonder Lab," *Metropolis*, December 1994.

40. Sinatra's work is sold through Legacy Recordings, a division of Sony Music.

41. On one occasion, the movie was an unnarrated visual of fly-over segments of the United States. Another film was of the surface of Mars.

42. Rebecca Segall, "The New Product Placement: Review of *Branded: The Buying and Selling of Teenagers*," *Nation*, February 23, 2003.

43. Ibid.

44. Martin and Siegel, letter to Sony Corporation of America, October 5, 2003.

45. National Coalition for the Homeless and National Law Center on Homelessness and Poverty, *Illegal to Be Homeless: The Criminalization of Homelessness in the United States*, 2002. A survey published by the National Coalition for the Homeless (NCH) reported that in 2002, one-third of the cities they examined prohibited lying down or sitting in particular public places. Between 1999 and 2002 there was a significant increase in laws that granted cities broad discretion to arrest homeless people. In 2002 more than one million families were on waiting lists for HUD-assisted housing. In New York the average waiting time for such housing was eight years, compared to a national average of three years. The most recent NCH report on the criminalization of the homeless can be found at http://www.nationalhomeless.org/crimreport/meanest.html

46. For more information on the criminalization of homeless people in public space, see Don Mitchell, "The Annihilation of Space by Law: The Roots and Implications of Anti-Homeless Laws in the United States," in *The Legal Geographies Reader: Law, Power, and Space*, ed. N. Blomley, D. Delaney, and R. T. Ford (Oxford, England: Blackwell Publishing, 2001); National Coalition for the Homeless and the National Law Center on Homelessness and Poverty, "Combating the Criminalization of Homelessness: A Guide to Understand and Prevent Legislation That Criminalizes Life-Sustaining Activities," 2002, http://www.nlchp.org/program_reportspubs.cfm?startRow=11&FA=4&TAB=0&prog=4 (access date May 15, 2007); National Coalition for the Homeless, "Illegal to Be Homeless: The Criminalization of Homelessness in the United States," 2004; J. McElroy, L. M. Takahashi, and S. Rowe, "The Sociospatial

Stigmatization of Homeless Women with Children," *Urban Geography* 23 (May–June 2002); John A. Powell and Marguerite L. Spencer, "Giving Them the Old 'One-Two': Gentrification and the K.O. of Impoverished Urban Dwellers of Color," *Howard Law Journal* (spring 2003).

47. Jonathan L. Hafetz, "Homeless Legal Advocacy: New Challenges and Directions for the Future," *Fordham Urban Law Journal* (2003), 1.

48. Kayden, New York Department of City Planning, and Municipal Art Society of New York, *Privately Owned Public Space*, 38.

49. Ibid., 284.

50. As Nancy Fraser reminds us, however, social equity and not simply access is central to public spheres. Whereas Habermas argued that one's social status could be "bracketed" so that people could interact as equals in public spheres, Fraser argues that this is impossible. Fraser, "Rethinking the Public Sphere."

51. I appreciate the help and suggestions of Thomas Martin and Mark Luehrs in developing this chapter, and for their information on the allegations against Sony.


## 6. Trump Tower and the Aesthetics of Largesse

1. *The Apprentice* Web site includes a virtual tour of the suite and gives instructions on how to purchase the furnishings and accessories. See http://www.trumponline.com/.

2. Nancy Franklin, "American Idol: For the Young Hopefuls on *The Apprentice*, Trump Towers," *New Yorker*, February 16, 2004.

3. The terminal is located on the west side of Twelfth Avenue between Forty-sixth and Fifty-fourth streets.

4. "Destination space is a high-quality public space that attracts employees, residents and visitors from outside, as well as from, the space's immediate neighborhood. Users will socialize, eat, shop, view art, or attend a programmed event, although they may also visit the space for sedentary, individual activities of reading and relaxing. The design supports a broad audience: spaces are usually sizable, well proportioned, brightly lit if indoors, aesthetically interesting, and constructed with first-class materials. Amenities are varied and frequently include some combination of food service, artwork, programmatic activities, restrooms, retail frontage and water features, as well as seating, tables, trees, and other plantings." Kayden, New York Department of City Planning, and Municipal Art Society of New York, *Privately Owned Public Space*, 49–50.

5. In *Privately Owned Public Space*, Kayden and his coauthors also note the existing confusion about the fact that there are spaces within Trump Tower that are "legally required to be open and accessible to the public."

6. For information about the five years of negotiations and deals that led to Trump's acquisition of the building site, see "Trump Pursued a 'Vision' of Tower with Tenacity," *New York Times*, August 26, 1980.

7. "Trump Tower," *Process Architecture: Economics [high-rise residences]*, monograph 64, 1986.

8. Tom Soter, "The Great Indoors," *Newsday*, January 16, 1993.

9. Ibid.

10. Paul Goldberger, "Architecture: Atrium of Trump Tower Is a Pleasant Surprise," *New York Times*, April 4, 1983.

11. Ibid.

12. Ibid.

13. Jonathan Mandell, *Trump Tower* (Secaucus, N.J.: Lyle Stuart, 1984), 18.

14. The subdistrict runs from East Thirty-third Street north to Central Park.

15. "The most widely used affirmative zoning technique is special district zoning. This technique permits areas with unique characteristics to flourish rather than be overwhelmed by standard development. The City Planning Commission has established special zoning districts to achieve specific planning and urban design objectives in a limited area. Each district stipulates requirements and/or provides zoning incentives for developers who provide the specific urban qualities the Commission seeks to promote in that area. It is a way of using private capital to carry out public policy." From Department of City Planning, *NYC Zoning Handbook: Special Zoning Districts*, chapter 11, July 1990, http://tenant.net/Other_Laws/zoning/zonch11 .html (accessed April 25, 2003).

16. Department of City Planning, *Zoning Handbook: A Guide to New York City's Zoning Resolution*, 2006.

17. Charles E. Tennant to Howard Zipser, November 25, 1983, Department of City Planning files.

18. Philip Schneider to Charles E. Tennant, January 25, 1984, Department of City Planning files.

19. Lisa Dunn to Donald Trump, Charles Smith, Phil Schneider, Norma Foerderer, and Ed Koch, August 9, 1984, Department of City Planning files.

20. Jan Levy to Martin Gallent, July 8, 1985, Department of City Planning files.

21. Charles E. Tennant to Donald Trump, January 24, 1984, Department of City Planning files.

22. Cited in Susan Leven, "Trump Tower and Trump Plaza," 1984, Department of City Planning files.

23. Mrs. Frank Langhammer to Donald Trump, December 15, 1984, Department of City Planning files.

24. Leven, "Trump Tower and Trump Plaza."

25. Cited in Albert Scardino, "Trump Finds Big 'Bonus' on 5th Avenue," *New York Times*, February 8, 1986.

26. "Trump Pursued a 'Vision' of Tower with Tenacity," *New York Times*.

27. Scardino, "Trump Finds Big 'Bonus' on 5th Avenue."

28. John Holusha, "Commercial Real Estate: Regional Market," *New York Times,* February 4, 2004.

29. Philip Schneider to Charles E. Tennant, April 10, 1984, Department of City Planning files.

30. Donald Trump to Philip Schneider, December 1984, Department of City Planning files.

31. Susan Heller and David Bird Anderson, "Occupational Hazards of the Atrium Set," *New York Times,* April 5, 1984.

32. Ibid. The article reported that the two businesspeople returned to the IBM Atrium.

33. Trump's lawsuit was successful because the judge found that the language of the abatement statute was vague regarding what an "underutilized property" was. See E. R. Shipp, "City's Denial of a Tax Break to Trump Is Ruled Improper," *New York Times,* December 15, 1982.

34. Cited in Mandell, *Trump Tower,* 9–10.

35. The two stores that the average shopper might visit, a convenience store and a record store, are both tucked into the basement.

36. Donald Trump, *Trumponline,* http://www.trumponline.com (accessed July 6, 2004).

37. Lloyd Grove with Elisa Lipsky-Karasz Grove, "Steamed Up at Fired Sign," *New York Daily News,* March 19, 2004.

38. South of Forty-ninth Street, retail rents were closer to $200 per square foot. Holusha, "Commercial Real Estate."

39. Arlene Holpp Scala and Jean Levitan, "Reality-Based Methods for Teaching Issues of Class and Privilege," *Transformations* 11, no. 1 (spring 2000).

40. Cited in Mandell, *Trump Tower,* 9.

41. Ada Louise Huxtable, "Architecture View," *New York Times,* July 1, 1979.

## Epilogue

1. Excellent work on public space after 9/11 can be found in several recent books and articles. See, for example, Setha M. Low, "The Memorialization of 9/11: Dominant and Local Discourses on the Rebuilding of the World Trade Center Site," *American Ethnologist* (photocopy of draft from the author, 2004); Michael Sorkin, *Starting from Zero: Reconstructing Downtown New York* (New York: Routledge, 2003); and Michael Sorkin and Sharon Zukin, *After the World Trade Center: Rethinking New York City* (New York: Routledge, 2002). Lynda Schneekloth gave one of the most compelling lectures on the question at the Conference for Educators in Landscape Architecture held September 25–28, 2002.

2. Recently, residents criticized the Environmental Protection Agency's handling of testing buildings near the WTC for toxins. See Anahad O'Conner, "Plan to Test Downtown Dust Draws Ire," *New York Times,* May 25, 2005.

3. William K. Rashbaum, "Safir Describes Security Plan for Times Sq.," *New York Times,* December 26, 1999.

4. Although researchers have noted an overall increase in security at other POPS, such as the Citibank Atrium and Sony Plaza, I have not seen the requests for identification and bag searches that these researchers noted in 2002 and 2003.

5. Two weeks after, on September 25, 2001, D.A.R.E. held an event at the Sony Arcade and honored then-chairman and CEO of Sony Music Entertainment, Thomas D. Mottola, for his "anti-drug campaign efforts throughout the music industry" (Sony Plaza donated the space for the event). Karen Kelso to Amanda Burden, April 24, 2003. A letter from the owner of Shallots (a restaurant adjacent to the Sony Plaza pedestrian space) dated September 20, 2001, requests a decision on the screens for seating while stating that their request seems "trivial" compared to everything that happened the week before.

6. *World Trade Center Site Rules and Regulations,* Port Authority of New York and New Jersey, 2006.

7. Jim Dwyer, "New York Police Covertly Join in at Protest Rallies," *New York Times,* December 22, 2005.

# Index

ABC, 64

access to public spaces: access to
processes that govern public spaces,
76–77, 91; codes of conduct and,
xx–xxi, 105–7, 110–14, 142–43;
corporate sorting of public life in
Sony Plaza, 98; limitations on, ix,
x, xviii; physical limitations on,
76, 91

advertising: importance of children to
advertisers, 110; Sony Plaza as
physical advertisement, 103–5; in
Times Square, 61–65. *See also*
marketing

aesthetics: aesthetic experience of
Trump Tower, 120, 122–36;
definition of, 146n5; role of, xxi

Afghanistan: bombing in 1998, 140;
invasion of, 140

AIDS and HIV: Americans' perceptions
of, 152n60; Giuliani's marginalization
of New Yorkers suffering from, 11–12,
17, 20–21, 150n30. *See also* Housing
Works

American Institute of Graphic Artists
conference: "Dangerous Ideas," 53

American Scenic and Historic
Preservation Society, 4–5

Anderson, David Bird, 167n31

Anderson, Pamela, 61, 64

*Apprentice, The* (TV), 117–18, 123, 136;
Web site, 165n1. *See also* Trump,
Donald

Art-in-Architecture program, GSA,
27–28. *See also* *Tilted Arc*

AT&T Building, 93–95, 162n6,
162n9; controversy at, 89–90;
distinctiveness of, 93; Johnson as

Dobnik, Verena, 161n2

Dunlap, David W., 162n9

Dunn, Christopher, 147n13, 150n25, 155n54

Dunn, Lisa, 166n19

Dwyer, Jim, 152n57, 168n7

*Economist,* 94

Eggers and Higgins, 26

Eisenberg, Arthur, 150n25

Elliot, Donald, 163n35

eminent domain: defined, 47–48; exercise of power of, in New York state, 156n7; lawsuits resulting from UDC's bid to use, 51–52; legislative process approving use of, in Times Square, 157n16; in New York Consolidated Laws, 48; property owners' right to fight against, 67; public interest undefined in law, 48; suggestions for streamlining process, 158n37; terms used in discourse of, 48–50, 156n12

Environmental Protection Agency, 167n2

Fahn, Charlotte, 160n16

Federal Building (New York), 27–28; offices in, 37

Federal Building (Oklahoma City): bombing in 1995, 40, 140

Federal Plaza, 22–44, 65; design history of, xviii; Jacob Javits Plaza and use of public space, xviii, 24–26, 34–44; maintaining fountain at, 27, 153n5; original design, 27; as public space, security issues and, 40–42; after September 11, 140; *Tilted Arc,* xviii, 24–34, 38, 40, 43, 153n1, 153n13, 154n19

Fenner, Austin, 155n51

Fifth Avenue subdistrict, 122–23. *See also* Trump Tower

Finkelpearl, Tom, 154n28

Finkelstein, Lola, 161n31

First Amendment, 7–8, 19, 22. *See also* free speech

Fish, Nicholas, 87, 161n28

*Flying Enterprise* (ship), 5–6

Francis, Mark, xiv, 147n10

Frank, Thomas, 157n24

Franklin, Nancy, 165n2

Fraser, Nancy, xvii, xviii, 1, 98, 145n2, 162n18, 165n50

free speech: front steps of New York's City Hall as site for, 3–22; Housing Works challenges to controls on, 10–22; relationships between public spaces and right to, xviii, 7–10

Freston, Tom, 105

General Services Administration (GSA), 31; Art-in-Architecture program, 27–28; commission for Federal Plaza sculpture, 27–29; security issue used in defending its control of Federal Plaza, 40–42; "use" versus "sculpture" argument against *Tilted Arc,* 29, 31–32

Gibson, Kristina, 146n3

Gilman, Sander L., 20, 152n58

Giuliani, Rudolph W., xi, xviii, 1, 3, 7, 149n16, 150n27; construction of his public image, 10, 20; importance of City Hall steps as site of representation for, 10; legal battles with Housing Works over steps of City Hall, 9–22; marginalization of New Yorkers suffering from AIDS/HIV, 11, 12, 17, 20–21, 150n30; New York Yankees Day celebration, 12–13, 150n30; "Next Phase of Quality

of Life: Creating a More Civil City"
speech (1996), 11–12, 149n19–20;
post–September 11 image, 3, 21–22;
rededication of refurbished *Statue of Justice*, 150n32; after September 11,
140
Glass House (Johnson), 161n4
Glenn, John, 16
Glimcher, Marc, 84, 88
Goldberger, Paul, 27, 93, 99–100,
120–21, 153n6, 161n1, 166n10
Goldstein, Barbara, 156n13
Goodgold, Sally, 162n22
graffiti: Giuliani's attitudes toward,
149n20
Grant, Peter, 157n20
Ground Zero, 141
Group of 35, 158n37
Grove, Elisa Lipsky-Karasz, 167n37
Grove, Lloyd, 167n37
GSA. *See* General Services
Administration
Gwathmey, Charles, 100
Gwathmey Siegel & Associates
Architects, 95

Haberman, Clyde, 149n12
Habermas, Jürgen, xvii, 145n2,
162n18
Hafetz, Jonathan L., 165n47
*Hague v. Committee for Industrial Organization*, 8
Hall, Peter, 157n21
Handelman, Stephen, 150n28
Hanly, Elizabeth, 164n39
Harris, Melissa, 161n31
Harvey, David, 147n9
Hawthorne, Christopher, 162n6
Heisel, Sylvia, 132
Heller, Susan, 167n31
Hénaff, Marcel, 147n12

Hess, Michael D., 151n52
Hilfiger, Tommy, 57
historic-preservation organizations,
156n4
HIV/AIDS. *See* AIDS and HIV
Holusha, John, 167n28, 167n38
Holzer, Harold, 52
homeless, the, xvi, 146n3;
criminalization of, 112, 115,
164n45–46; exclusion from Sony
Plaza, 105–7, 112–14; legal battles of
Housing Works over steps of City
Hall regarding, 9–22; restrictive
codes of conduct and campaign
against, xxi
Horowitz, Gregg M., 153n13
Housing Works, xviii, 3, 7, 149n17,
151n40; cost to city of May 2005
ruling in favor of, 19, 22, 152n57;
criticisms against Giuliani, 11–12, 17,
20–21; government contracts to
provide housing and services to
people with HIV/AIDS, Giuliani's
cuts to, 19–20; legal battles over the
steps of City Hall, 9–22; World AIDS
Day event, 15–16, 18, 21
*Housing Works, Inc. v. Safir*, 150n24,
150n31
*Housing Works v. Kerik*, 152n56
*How to Turn a Place Around: A Handbook for Creating Successful Public Spaces* (Project for Public
Spaces), xiv
Huxtable, Ada Louise, 45, 137, 167n41

IBM, 94, 159n9
IBM Atrium, xx, 71–91; bamboo tree
grove in, 73–74, 80–83; controversy
over proposed changes to, 73–76,
81–85; exterior of, 78; failure to
comply with provisions for

management of sculpture display, 87–89; IBM's diminishing care for, 81, 83, 160n18; new owner with new agenda, 81–87; original contract and original design, 75, 77–81; plan view of, 80; postrenovation conflict over, 87–89; relationship to office tower, 78–79; removal of a few stands of bamboo, effect of, 74, 84; after renovation (2001), 76; reviews on first opening, 73–74; value of bonus square footage built in return for, 77
IBM Building: after September 11, 141
Impellitteri, Vincent R., 5
individual rights: broad changes to U.S. domestic policies regarding, xxi–xxii
Infoquest, 95, 104–5, 162n12
interior public spaces, xx–xxii. *See also* IBM Atrium; Sony Plaza; Trump Tower

Jacob Javits Plaza, xviii, 26, 34–44; critical responses to, 34–39; description of, 25, 34; difficulty of designing public space in New York addressed by, 37–39; eating lunch as one use of, 35–36; limitations of physical layout and design, 37; plan view of, 39; "publics" using, 37, 43; renaming of Federal Plaza to, 24; Schwartz's 1997 American Society of Landscape Architects Award for, 35; after September 11, 140. *See also* Federal Plaza
Jacobs, Carrie, 155n53
Jefferson, Thomas, 4
Johnson, Philip, 52, 93, 100–101, 156n5, 157n18, 161n1; AT&T Building, 93–95, 162n6, 162n9; projects of, 161n5

Kahn and Jacobs, 26
Kalman, Tibor, xix, 52–56, 60–61, 64, 66, 68, 140, 157n24, 158n37
Karp, Ivan C., 82, 160n13
Katz, Cindy, 147n15
Kayden, Jerold, 71–73, 145n1, 148n19, 159n1, 161n24, 162n19, 165n4–5, 165n48
Kelso, Karen, 168n5
Kennedy, John F., 28
Kimmelman, Michael, 153n12
King, Charles, 12, 17–18
Klein, Naomi, 95, 104, 148n20
Koch, Edward, 4, 47, 117, 125, 137, 148n5

Lambert, Bruce, 159n5
land value: pricing out existing residents and, xiv
Langhammer, Mrs. Frank, 126, 166n23
League of Urban Landscape Architects, 100
Leval, Pierre N. (judge), 152n56
Leven, Susan, 126, 166n22
Levine, Caroline, 153n13
Levitan, Jean, 136–37, 167n39
Levy, Jan, 166n20
Lieberman, Marc, 132
Light, Andrew, 147n12
Lindsay, John, 4
Local Law 49, 12
locations of free speech: "charged" vs. "marginal," 9
Low, Setha M., 146n3, 146n4, 167n1
Lower Manhattan Development Corporation (LMDC), 142
Luehrs, Mark, 112

Mandell, Jonathan, 166n13
Mangin, Joseph, 3

marketing: children as target market of Sony, 104–5, 107–10; at Sony Plaza, 104–5; stealth, 164n38

*Martha Schwartz: Transfiguration of Commonplace,* 34

Martin, Thomas, 112–13

Maziarz, George D., 158n36

McCobb, Patricia, 100, 162n21

McComb, John, Jr., 3, 148n2

McElroy, Jaime, 164n46

McGregor, David, 91, 161n36

Mele, Christopher, xiv, 146n8

Merker, Kyle, 160n22

Merrifield, Andy, 147n9

Messinger, Ruth, 89, 161n33, 161n35

*Metropolis Magazine,* 61

Meyer, Elizabeth K., 37, 154n38

Microsoft, 64

Mies van der Rohe, Ludwig, 161n5

millennium celebration security plan for Times Square, 141

Miller, Kristine, 148n16–17

Minor, Judge, 152n56

Minskoff, Edward J., 73–76, 81–85, 87–89, 135, 160n14, 161n28

Mitchell, Don, 8, 146n3, 147n14, 164n46

"mixed use" building: Trump Tower as, 133

modifications: major versus minor, 84–85, 89–90, 162n22

Mondale, Joan, 154n19

morality of New Times Square: creating, 51, 60–61, 69

Motherwell, Robert, 28

Mottola, Thomas D., 105, 168n5

MTV, 64

Municipal Art Society (MAS), 72, 74, 83, 89, 145n1, 156n5; mission of, 159n4

Muschamp, Herbert, 77–78

museum: Infoquest in AT&T Building, 95, 104–5, 162n12; Sony Wonder Technology Lab as, 98, 102–3, 105, 107–10, 163n32, 164n39

My First Sony products, 105

Nadal, Luc, 147n12

*Nation,* 110

National Coalition for Homeless, 164n45–46

National Law Center on Homelessness and Poverty (NLCHP), 112, 164n45–46

NBC, 64

New Amsterdam Theater, 156n4, 158n34

New Jersey Casino Control Commission, 135–36

New London (Connecticut): eminent-domain case in, 67

*Newsday,* 120

New Times Square, 45, 46; advertisements in, 61–65; creating morality of, 51, 60–61, 69; creation of new image for, 54, 56–61, 65; kinds of tenants choosing to locate in, 53–54; new public for, 60–61. *See also* Times Square

New Year's Eve in Times Square: security for, 45, 141

New York City: Division of AIDS Services, 12, 17–18; Planning Department, xix, xx, 105; public life bound by regulation and codes of conduct, x; as uniquely familiar, ix

New York Civil Liberties Union (NYCLU), 7, 151n40; First Amendment cases against Giuliani involving, 12–13, 16–20

New York Consolidated Laws, 48, 49, 156n7

*Privately Owned Public Space: The New York City Experience* (Kayden), 71–72, 86, 165n5

private space: public investment in, 119–21, 136–37

Project for Public Spaces (PPS), xiv, xvi, 84; mission of, 146n6

property owners: lawsuits resulting from UDC's bid to use eminent domain in Times Square, 51–52; right to fight against eminent domain, 67

psychologists: advertising and marketing using expertise of, 110

public(s), the: controls on who appears as part of, 20–21, 33; denizens of Times Square edited to transform, 58–61; of Jacob Javits Plaza, 37, 43; target markets at Sony Plaza and, 104–5; of Times Square, 47–49; of WTC site, 141–43

public and appropriate use: permanent form given to GSA-approved definition of, 35, 39

public art, 157n26. *See also Tilted Arc*

public forum, traditional, 8; rules set up governing, 9; steps of City Hall as, 2–3, 152n56

public interest, the: condemnation in, 47–69; reasons for use of eminent domain on Forty-second Street in, 48–52; renovation of IBM Atrium in, argument for, 82

public investment in private space, 136–37

public involvement in decision making, xv, 85, 91

public ownership, ix–xi

public/private partnerships managing public spaces, 146n3

*Public Space* (Carr et al.), xiv–xv

public space(s), xiii–xvi; criminalization of homeless people in, 112, 115, 164n45–46; defining, ix–xvii, 154n33; design-based studies of, xiii–xvi; destination space, 165n4; dynamic nature of, 32; essential and obvious characteristics, ix–xi; forms of restricting access to, x; lack of legal definition of, 113, 147n13; litigating for access to, 113; methodological lenses used to understand, xii; normative definition of, xi; Patriot Act and idea of "right" to, xxi–xxii, 143–44; preoccupation with enduring physical qualities of, xi; private spaces linked to, through public policy, 21; September 11 impact on, xxi, 139–44, 167n1; as site for democratic action, ix, xi–xii, xvi–xvii, 19–20, 32–33; as tenuous condition, x, xi; trade-offs of linking commercial spaces and, 110; value of interior, 114–16

public space–public sphere hybrid, xii, xvi, xvii; litigation required to maintain, 3, 10–22

public sphere(s), 145n2; definition of, xvii; generated by *Tilted Arc*, 26–34; producing, xv; social equity as central to, 165n50; transnational, xvii, 145n2

"public use" argument against *Tilted Arc*, 29–30

Quinn, Christine, 151n45

Rashbaum, William K., 168n3
Rauschenberg, Robert, 82
Re, Edward D., 29, 33, 40
*Reconstructing Times Square: Politics and Culture in Urban Development* (Reichl), 47

Sony Atrium, 79

Sony Corporation, 89; stealth
marketing by, 164n38

Sony Ericsson Mobile Communications,
164n38

Sony Music, 105

Sony Plaza, xi, xx–xxi, 93–116; BB the
Wonderbot, 103–4, 107–8, 110, 141,
163n31; codes of conduct, xx–xxi,
105–7, 110–14; inside, 102–3;
materials used in design of, 102–3;
modifications, 95–98, 162n22; as
physical advertisement, 103–5; plan of
bonus spaces, 99; public museums
and target markets, 103–14; public
space calculus, 98–102; after
September 11, 141

Sony Wonder Technology Lab, 98,
102–3, 105, 163n32, 164n39; visiting,
107–10

Sorkin, Michael, xv, xvi, 66, 68,
159n40, 167n1

Soter, Tom, 166n8

special district zoning, 166n15

Special Midtown District: Fifth Avenue
as subdistrict of, 122–23

speech: graffiti as form of, 149n20. *See
also* free speech

Spencer, Marguerite L., 165n46

Staeheli, Lynn, 146n3

*Starting from Zero* (Sorkin), 12

stealth marketing, 164n38

Stern, Robert M., 52–53

Stern, William, 45–46

Stetson, Damon, 153n7

Stone, Andrew M., xiv, 147n10

Storr, Robert, 153n9

Strong, Tracy B., 147n12

Sturtz, Herbert, 163n35

Supreme Court, 67, 157n16

Swanke Hayden Connell Architects, 120

Takahashi, Lois M., 164n46

tax abatements for Trump Tower, 133,
167n33

Tennant, Charles E., 166n17, 166n21

Tiffany's, 126

*Tilted Arc* (Serra), xviii, 24, 26–34, 43,
153n1, 153n13; art historians on, 31–34;
criticism as central to history of,
33–34; debates over, 29, 154n19;
demolition of, 28–29, 40; description
of, 25, 28; hearing over relocation of,
29–33; opponents of, 29–30; plan
view of, 38; site-specific nature of,
30–31; supporters of, 30–31, 33

time, location, and manner doctrine to
limit speech acts, 9

Times Square, 45–69; combination of
moral, legal, and design arguments
transforming, 46–47, 49–51, 69;
condemnation in public's interest,
47–69; construction site (1998), 55;
demolition and the public's interest,
47; "economic potential" of, UDC's
arguments for increasing, 51;
eminent domain used in, 48–52,
157n16; historic preservation in,
155n4; iconic status of, 45–46; image
of, as dirty and dangerous, 50; map
of, 50; poster campaign giving
impression of transformation, 56–61,
65; proposals for, 52–56; publics of,
47–49; redevelopment effect on the
public of, x, 67–68; redevelopment
of, xviii; renaming to "the New
Times Square," 45; after September
11, 140–41; sex business in, 51, 62,
67–68

Times Square Business Improvement
District, 155n1; mission statement
of, 157n29; *Report on the Secondary
Effects of Concentration of Adult Use*

**180**

**Kristine F. Miller** is associate professor of landscape architecture at the University of Minnesota.